GUIDE FOR CELEBRATING®
CHRISTIAN INITIATION
WITH CHILDREN

PREPARING PARISH WORSHIP™

RITA BURNS SENSEMAN
VICTORIA M. TUFANO
PAUL TURNER
D. TODD WILLIAMSON

LTP
LITURGY
TRAINING
PUBLICATIONS

Nihil Obstat
Very Reverend Daniel A. Smilanic, JCD
Vicar for Canonical Services
Archdiocese of Chicago
July 30, 2016

Imprimatur
Very Reverend Ronald A. Hicks
Vicar General
Archdiocese of Chicago
July 30, 2016

The *Nihil Obstat* and *Imprimatur* are declarations that the material is free from doctrinal or moral error, and thus is granted permission to publish in accordance with c. 827. No legal responsibility is assumed by the grant of this permission. No implication is contained herein that those who have granted the *Nihil Obstat* and *Imprimatur* agree with the content, opinions, or statements expressed.

This book was edited by Mary Fox, Víctor R. Pérez was the production editor, Anna Manhart was the series designer, Juan Alberto Castillo was the cover designer, and Kari Nicholls was the production artist.

Cover photo by Danielle A. Noe, MDIV. Photos on pages 8, 11, 18, 91–94, 116, 120, 128 by Karen Callaway; page 95 by David Kamba © LTP; pages 10, 60, 64, 75, 83, 86, 89, 112–113 by Andrew Kennedy Lewis © LTP; page 7 by Carl F. Mengeling; page 90 © Antonio Pérez; and pages 9, 24, 31–36, 38, 46, 57, 77, 97, 100 and 101 © John Zich.

Art on page vii © Martin Erspamer, OSB.

GUIDE FOR CELEBRATING® CHRISTIAN INITIATION WITH CHILDREN © 2017 Archdiocese of Chicago: Liturgy Training Publications, 3949 South Racine Avenue, Chicago, IL 60609, 1-800-933-1800; fax 1-800-933-7094; e-mail orders@ltp.org. All rights reserved. See our website at www.LTP.org.

This book is part of the *Preparing Parish Worship*™ series.

21 20 19 18 17   1 2 3 4 5

Printed in the United States of America.

Library of Congress Control Number: 2016954110

ISBN 978-1-61671-315-7

EGCCIC

CONTENTS

PREFACE

Zachary tripped as his brother Elias playfully pushed him aside, rushing past him on the road.

"Don't lose your way, Zachary!" Elias laughed. Turning, he called to his wife and children, "Hurry up. The rabbi is already speaking." Elias' family quickly passed Zachary and his family on the road.

Zachary fumed. "Leave him alone," Esther said soothingly to her husband. "What does it matter if he gets there first?"

Yet, somehow, it mattered. All through his life, Zachary had put up with his younger brother. Elias was smarter, more athletic, and better looking. Good fortune followed Elias everywhere. His crops again this year were absolutely robust. Zachary could not even feed and clothe his children the way Elias took care of his family. Zachary was a faithful son of Abraham. This just wasn't fair.

Esther could see the old jealousy in her husband's eyes. "Elias is just having fun. Let it go," she stressed. "Come on, kids," she called out, and the youngsters quickly caught up with their parents.

The crowd came into view before Zachary and Esther could hear the rabbi's words. "I've never seen this many people. Anywhere," marveled Zachary. "Not even at the festival. Is this why you wanted to bring the children?"

"Not exactly. I've heard that this rabbi is a very holy man." She turned softly toward Zachary. "I want him to bless our children."

When they heard the rabbi's voice, they could tell that they had entered the presence of a gifted preacher. "He speaks with authority, and not like our scribes,"[1] Zachary said to Esther. "What's his name again?"

"Jesus," she said, and Zachary looked at her more closely now, because her voice possessed a warmth he normally heard only when she spoke about him.

Jesus was taking a question from a Pharisee. "Is it lawful for a husband to divorce his wife?"[2]

---

1. Mark 1:22.
2. Mark 10:2.

Jesus said, "They are no longer two, but one flesh."[3]

Zachary was alarmed. "Look at all the kids here," he said. "Why is that guy asking about divorce?"

Just then Zachary's children spotted their cousins. His oldest ran up to Elias' children and tagged the youngest. "You're it!" he declared and dashed away.

All the kids then started running around the back side of the crowd. Zachary needed to get their attention, but he did not want to anger those who were listening to the rabbi. He whispered loudly to his kids, "Children! Children, come back!" But it was too late. Zachary's children disappeared into the thick of the crowd. Leaving their cousins behind and bewildered, they squirmed their way to the very front, where they suddenly found themselves in the open space between the crowd and the rabbi.

Zachary and Esther started pushing their way to the front. "Excuse us. Excuse us, please," they said. They even brushed past Elias. "Where do you think you're going?" the younger brother sneered. But the parents kept muscling their way to the front when they suddenly heard two voices like thunder.

"Get out of here," commanded James the son of Zebedee. "What are you kids doing here?" asked James' brother John.

Esther pressed her way to the front, her face flushed. "Excuse them," she smiled. Her kids ran back to her, frightened, seeking her protection. Esther continued, "But while we're here," she said, placing her hands tenderly behind the heads of her children, "I was hoping . . ."

"Please keep an eye on your children," interrupted James. "This is not the place for them."[4]

"Oh, but it is," said the rabbi.

James and John looked irritated at Jesus. How could they keep order if he kept undermining their authority?

"Let the children come to me." Now Jesus sounded annoyed. "Do not prevent them."[5]

Zachary knew what Esther wanted, but he felt embarrassed. Surely Jesus was going to ask for a donation. He had nothing. He had no coins, no food, no animals—nothing that he could give a rabbi for blessing his children. He

---

3. Mark 10:8.
4. Mark 10:13.
5. Mark 10:14.

GUIDE FOR CELEBRATING® CHRISTIAN INITIATION WITH CHILDREN

humbly realized that his younger brother could do this much better. Elias possessed many things.

Then Jesus fixed his gaze, first on James and John, and then directly at Zachary, as if reading the man's thoughts about living in poverty. Indicating the children, Jesus said, "The kingdom of God belongs to such as these."[6]

"It *belongs* to them?" wondered Zachary out loud. His children owned nothing. How could they possibly own a kingdom?

"Amen, I say to you," continued Jesus, "whoever does not accept the kingdom of God like a child will not enter it."[7]

Zachary wondered again, "But children have nothing. How can they enter a kingdom?"

Without any further prompting, Zachary's children left Esther behind and ran into the arms of Jesus. The rabbi bent down and embraced them all. Esther had never spoken her request out loud, but in amazement she saw her hopes fulfilled. Jesus placed his hands on the children, and he blessed them.[8]

Elias watched it all with suspicion. As he parted ways with his younger brother, Zachary called out, "Don't lose your way, Elias."

Throughout his ministry, Jesus surprised many people by his pastoral outreach to people on the margins—tax collectors, prostitutes, and even children. Today people still sometimes marvel at what mere children are able to possess: the treasures of the Kingdom of Heaven.

—Paul Turner

---

6. Mark 10:14.
7. Mark 10:15.
8. Mark 10:16.

WELCOME

It was not so long ago that Catholic life for children was predictable. They were baptized within a few weeks of birth, attended a Catholic school or religious-education program, made their first Communion in second grade, and received Confirmation sometime in adolescence, depending on the diocesan practice. Maybe they went to a Catholic high school or at least joined the parish teen group. Perhaps they met a nice Catholic boy or girl at their Catholic college, Newman Center, or young adults' group at the parish, got married, and had children, who were baptized within a few weeks of birth. The circle of Catholic life. The way it had always been.

Your experience may lead you to question whether that was the way it has always been. Certainly, it is not the way it is now. If you are a priest, deacon, coordinator of a Christian initiation team, a director of religious education, or a catechist, you know that children receive the initiation sacraments at varied ages. At your parish, some children are baptized as infants, while other families seek Baptism for a child who is in elementary school. Sometimes a child in grade school or a teenager requests Baptism for him or herself. You may

> The three sacraments of initiation closely combine to bring us, the faithful of Christ, to his full stature and to enable us to carry out the mission of the entire people of God in the Church and in the world.
>
> —*Christian Initiation*, General Introduction, 2

be aware, too, that the order of the celebration of the sacraments varies. Perhaps in yours or a neighboring diocese, Confirmation is celebrated before children receive first Communion. And if you have participated at an Easter Vigil in which children of catechetical age were baptized, you observed that they were confirmed and received first Eucharist at the same liturgy.

When you read the chapter "The Theological and Historical Developments of the Full Initiation of Children," by Paul Turner, on page 1–15 of this book, you will learn that the reception of the sacraments has not followed the same order during every age. You will find that in the early Church children and adults were confirmed after Baptism and then welcomed to the

Eucharistic table. As you will discover in that chapter, the *Rite of Christian Initiation of Adults* (RCIA) has restored that practice for both adults and children of catechetical age. Now when these children and adults are baptized, they also are confirmed and receive Communion at that liturgy. Usually this occurs at the Easter Vigil.

The truth is many unbaptized children who have reached catechetical age come to us for initiation. Often, parishes struggle with how to meet the needs of these families. Parish ministers may wonder how these children should be accompanied on their journey of initiation. Some may be unsure if the children should participate in the rituals that are part of the *Rite of Christian Initiation of Adults*. And sometimes there is discomfort with the provision in the RCIA that children of catechetical age are to receive all the initiation sacraments at the same liturgy. For all of these concerns, the Church provides guidance in the *Rite of Christian Initiation of Adults*, Part II, chapter 1, "Christian Initiation of Children Who Have Reached Catechetical Age." Here we find that the process of initiation for children is marked by liturgical rites adapted to their age and spiritual growth.

About This Book

This book will help you prepare and celebrate the rites of the Christian initiation journey in ways that are appropriate for children. Sometimes the book goes beyond just looking at the rites to offer pastoral suggestions for dealing with children and their families and discerning what is right for a particular situation. This book also offers assistance in discerning the path for baptized children who have received no catechetical formation, and for baptized children from other Christian communities who wish to be received into the full communion of the Catholic Church.

Whether you are a coordinator of Christian initiation or director of liturgy, faith formation, or religious education, a priest, deacon, catechist, or member of the initiation team, this *Guide for Celebrating® Christian Initiation with Children* will enrich your understanding of the initiation process. This book provides background on the history and theology of Christian initiation and walks you through the many rites that lead to the sacraments of initiation. The guidance the resource gives will ensure smooth preparation for each liturgical rite. Frequently asked questions about the initiation of children, the role of parents during the process, and the place of religious-education programs will be answered.

It would be helpful to the reader of this book to have a copy of the RCIA at hand. Please notice that the initials RCIA will be used in this book only to refer to the ritual text. The journey of those coming to faith will be called the initiation process, or the catechumenal process, or the catechumenal journey, or other such terms.

About the Authors

RITA BURNS SENSEMAN is director of religious education at St. Benedict Parish in Terre Haute, Indiana. She is also a freelance writer who has written books and articles on various aspects of the *Rite of Christian Initiation of Adults* and the sacraments of initiation, including a Confirmation preparation program, *Anointed in the Spirit*, (Winona, Minnesota: St. Mary's Press, 2010). Rita formerly was associate director of catechetics/religious education in the Archdiocese of Detroit. She was a team member of the North American Forum on the Catechumenate and is currently a contributor for the website TeamRCIA. She has been involved in initiation and catechetical ministry for more than thirty years and holds a master of arts in theological studies from the University of Notre Dame.

VICTORIA M. TUFANO is senior editor and liturgical consultant at Liturgy Training Publications. She has served as a parish director of liturgy and Christian initiation and as a diocesan director of worship. She was a team member for institutes of the North American Forum on the Catechumenate and served on Forum's board of directors. She is a frequent writer and speaker on liturgy and Christian initiation, and was the editor of *Catechumenate: A Journal of Christian Initiation* and of several books on initiation. She holds a master of arts in liturgical studies and a master of divinity, both from the University of Notre Dame.

PAUL TURNER is pastor of St. Anthony Parish in Kansas City, Missouri. A priest of the Diocese of Kansas City-St. Joseph, he holds a doctorate in sacred theology from Sant'Anselmo in Rome. His publications include *At the Supper of the Lamb* (Chicago: Liturgy Training Publications, 2011); *Glory in the Cross* (Collegeville, Minnesota: Liturgical Press, 2011); *ML Bulletin Inserts* (San Jose: Resource Publications, 2012); and *Celebrating Initiation: A Guide for Priests* (Chicago: World Library Publications, 2008). He is a former president of the North American Academy of Liturgy and a member of *Societas Liturgica* and the Catholic Academy of Liturgy. He is the 2013 recipient of the Jubilate Deo Award (National Association of Pastoral Musicians) and the Frederick McManus Award (Federation of Diocesan Liturgical Commissions). He serves as a facilitator for the International Commission on English in the Liturgy. Fr. Turner has provided the prefacep and the chapter "The Theological and Historical Developments of the Full Christian Initiation of Children."

D. TODD WILLIAMSON is the director of the Office for Divine Worship in the Archdiocese of Chicago. He holds a master of theological studies from Catholic Theological Union, in Chicago. He is the author of two editions of *Sourcebook for Sundays, Seasons, and Weekdays: The Almanac for Pastoral Liturgy* (2007 and 2008), and has contributed to subsequent editions. He has also written for numerous periodicals, including *Rite, Pastoral Liturgy, Catechumenate: A Journal of Christian Initiation,* and *Religion Teacher's Journal.* He is the author, with Joe Paprocki, of *Great Is the Mystery: Encountering the Formational Power of Liturgy* (Chicago: Liturgy Training Publications, 2013). Todd also is a teacher and national speaker in the areas of liturgy and the sacraments.

The Theological and Historical Developments of the Full Christian Initiation of Children

> For the promise is made to you and to your children and
> to all those far off, whomever the Lord our God will call.
>
> —Acts of the Apostles 2:39

Just as good parents provide for the needs of children born into their family, so does the Church. Throughout the ages of Christian history the Church has offered sacraments of initiation to children. The practice has changed according to the sensibilities of times and cultures, but the Church has consistently expressed a parental solicitude for children.

All the sacraments participate in divine grace. In fact, God acts first. God's grace offers salvation to all.[1] Through the sacraments, the Church welcomes children to participation in the divine life of Christ. The full initiation of children is a response to God's gracious invitation.

It has been that way from the beginning of Christian history.

Scripture

The New Testament offers no clear evidence for the Baptism of Children or for their reception of Communion. However, there is circumstantial evidence for both practices.

The Acts of the Apostles contains several reports of Baptisms, some in great numbers, others in small groups. The book offers a discernible pattern of household Baptisms. Crispus, a synagogue official, and his household became believers and were baptized after hearing the preaching of St. Paul.[2] Lydia and her household did the same.[3] Paul and Silas walked out of prison

---

1. Titus 2:11.
2. Acts 18:8.
3. Acts 16:11–15.

1

after an earthquake loosened their chains.[4] The jailer responsible for their care came to faith after observing their miraculous release. He and his entire household were baptized.[5] Peter was preaching to the household of Cornelius when the gathered assembly started manifesting gifts of the Holy Spirit. Peter ordered the Baptism of them all.[6]

Outside of Acts similar evidence persists. St. Paul admits to performing Baptisms on only one occasion—for the household of Stephanas.[7] In John's Gospel account, after Jesus cured the son of a royal official, the man and all in his household believed in Jesus.[8] Although this event predates testimony of Christian Baptism, all of which followed the Resurrection, the belief that attracted an entire household fits this pattern.

None of these reports explicitly states that children were among the members of the household. But it is hard to imagine that they were not, harder still to imagine parents agreeing that small children in their house were too young to be baptized. Even in the stories about large group Baptisms, such as three thousand persons on the day of Pentecost,[9] it is hard to imagine that the Apostles solicitously excluded the youngest among them, especially since Peter had just explicitly promised the gift of the Holy Spirit to his listeners and to their children.[10]

> Believe in the Lord Jesus and you and your household will be saved.
> —Acts of the Apostles 16:31

Concerning family life, Paul took up the problem of believers marrying unbelievers. He said that the believer made the unbelieving spouse holy, and their children were holy.[11] This offers no explicit mention of Baptism, but the pastoral concern for the spiritual lives of children is evident.

Furthermore, Paul compared Baptism to the Jewish ceremony of circumcision.[12] Although he was making the broader point that adult Gentile converts need not be circumcised, Paul thought of Baptism as a ceremony that borrows significance from a Jewish rite normally performed on infants.

---

4. Acts 16:26.
5. Acts 16:29–33.
6. Acts 10:44, 47.
7. 1 Corinthians 1:16.
8. John 4:46b, 53b.
9. Acts 2:41.
10. Acts 2:39.
11. 1 Corinthians 7:14.
12. Colossians 2:11–12.

In general, Jesus showed interest in children as he did for others marginalized in society. He forbade people to keep children from him and said that one enters the Kingdom of God like a child.[13] He said that those who welcomed a child welcomed him.[14]

Regarding Communion in the New Testament, Paul writes about the practice of combining the Lord's Supper with the community meal.[15] He also considered the practice of prophetic utterances when the whole Church came together.[16] It is unclear if children participated in these ecclesial gatherings, but where else would they go? If families included believers, certainly children participated as they were able.

In summary, the New Testament describes an environment in which children were welcomed and households were baptized. The Lord's Supper was shared among believers who sometimes combined it with a community meal. Surely there was room for children.

Early Church History

Clear evidence for the Baptism of infants surfaced by the end of the second century. Origen of Alexandria (†253) favored the practice.[17] Tertullian of Carthage (†220) objected to it.[18] However, Cyprian of Carthage (†258) supported baptizing infants immediately after their birth.[19] The *Apostolic Tradition* (3rd–4th c.) describes an elaborate initiation ceremony in which catechumens were baptized, anointed, and given Communion. During the liturgy, the first among them to participate in all these ceremonies were infants too young to speak or walk.[20]

Like the *Apostolic Tradition*, Cyprian clearly indicates that infants also received Communion.[21] From the very earliest generations of Christians, therefore, the full initiation of children was well established.

By the fifth century, when bishops baptized, they also anointed and offered Communion to the same candidates, no matter their age. But a separate

---

13. Mark 10:14–15; Matthew 19:14–15; Luke 18:16–17.
14. Luke 9:48; Matthew 18:3–5.
15. 1 Corinthians 11:17–21.
16. 1 Corinthians 14:22–25.
17. Paul Turner, *Ages of Initiation: The First Two Christian Millennia* (Collegeville: Liturgical Press, 2000): [CD-ROM] chapter 2, part 7.
18. Turner, *Ages of Initiation*, ch. 2, pt. 7.
19. Turner, *Ages of Initiation*, ch. 2, pt. 7.
20. Turner, *Ages of Initiation*, ch. 2, pt. 7.
21. Turner, *Ages of Initiation*, ch. 2, pt. 8.

ceremony developed for bishops to confirm those who had been baptized by other ministers. Although priests and deacons retained the permission to baptize, Confirmation was reserved to a bishop. Priests and deacons gave Communion to the infants they baptized. It was considered part of their initiation rites, inseparably coupled to their Baptism.[22]

This persisted when the Church began to develop sacramentaries and orders of worship. For example, the Gallican Order XV (775–780) explained that a priest who baptized also gave Communion to all present, including the infants he had just baptized. Confirmation would wait until a bishop became available.[23]

When bishops baptized infants in the Middle Ages, they continued to offer full initiation. For example, the *Roman Pontifical* of the twelfth century gives explicit instructions for the bishop to baptize, confirm, and give Communion to infants.[24]

A canon in the Fourth Lateran Council (1215) called for all to confess their sins at least once a year, beginning at the years of discretion.[25] This contributed to the pastoral practice of deferring first Communion from the baptismal ceremony to a later age. Because bishops were confirming so few infants at Baptism, the celebration of Confirmation was generally deferred from Baptism as well. Consequently, the gradual breakup of the unified initiation ceremony became complete by the thirteenth century. However, for well over a thousand years the practice of giving Communion to infants endured in the Church, and bishops administered all three initiation sacraments together to children when they baptized.

Only after the Protestant Reformation in the early sixteenth century did the Church establish a minimum age for Confirmation.[26] The Reformation uncovered a catechetical crisis in the Church. The publication of the *Catechism of the Council of Trent* addressed this need. Its appearance in 1566 preceded the beginning of Trent's liturgical reform by four years, which shows that the bishops perceived that catechetical needs outweighed liturgical needs. Although catechetical preparation for Confirmation was fairly minimal, it provided some opportunity to educate the faithful on the basics of their faith. The

---

22. Turner, *Ages of Initiation*, ch. 4.
23. Turner, *Ages of Initiation*, ch. 5, part 7.
24. Turner, *Ages of Initiation*, ch. 7, pt. 1.
25. Turner, *Ages of Initiation*, ch. 8, pt. 5.
26. Turner, *Ages of Initiation*, ch. 9, pt. 6.

sequence of receiving Confirmation and first Communion had more to do with the availability of the bishop than any catechetical plan.

First Communion ceremonies became popular as a grassroots effort starting in the late sixteenth century. They spread as the inspirational celebration that concluded religious formation for children. Consequently, by the seventeenth century it was typical for a child to experience the initiation rites in this way: Baptism in infancy by the local priest, Confirmation around age seven or higher when the bishop came to town, and first Communion when completing catechesis around the age of ten or fourteen.[27]

The Post-Reformation Church

By the nineteenth century, some regional Church councils took up the question of the sequence of Confirmation and first Communion. Some preferred having Confirmation follow first Communion. For example, in 1850 the Council of Sens in France said that after first Communion, children would have more intelligence and piety, and could receive Confirmation more fruitfully.[28] Others, however, argued the reverse. Whenever Rome spoke on the situation, it consistently favored young ages for first Communion[29] and Confirmation. In 1897 Pope Leo XIII explicitly requested that Confirmation precede first Communion faithfully and perpetually.[30]

The catechesis and celebration of first Communion changed considerably under Pope Pius X when the Vatican's Sacred Congregation of the Discipline of Sacraments issued *Quam singulari* in 1910. This permitted children to receive Communion at the age of reason, or about the seventh year, which would include age six.[31] This caused considerable upheaval in the pastoral practice of preparing children for sacraments.[32] Because the new document said nothing about Confirmation,

> It is clear that the age of discretion for receiving Holy Communion is that at which the child knows the difference between the Eucharistic Bread and ordinary, material bread.
>
> —*Quam singulari*

---

27. Turner, *Ages of Initiation*, ch. 10, pts. 5 and 8.
28. Turner, *Ages of Initiation*, ch. 11, pt. 9.
29. Turner, *Ages of Initiation*, ch. 11, pt. 5.
30. Turner, *Ages of Initiation*, ch. 11, pt. 10.
31. Turner, *Ages of Initiation*, ch. 12, pt. 3.
32. Turner, *Ages of Initiation*, ch. 12, pt. 4.

some bishops eventually began raising the age of Confirmation in their dioceses. This provided a sacrament to accompany the completion of religious education, filling a void that the younger age of first Communion had left behind.

Throughout the twentieth century, priests gradually received permission to administer Confirmation in exceptional circumstances.[33] In 1929 the number of converts in Latin America had multiplied so exponentially beyond the availability of bishops that Pope Pius IX gave bishops permission to appoint priests to confirm. (It is still possible to find some places in Latin America where the Confirmation of infants is practiced.) In 1946 most priests received the faculty to confirm infants and adults in danger of death. This permission endures: a priest who baptizes an infant in danger of death also has the faculty to confirm that same infant.[34] In 1947 bishops in mission territories received permission to allow all their priests to confirm in the absence of the bishop.

When the post-Vatican II *Rite of Christian Initiation of Adults* was published, it permitted any priest to confirm in the same ceremony the adults and children of catechetical age whom he baptized.[35] This was confirmed in the 1983 *Code of Canon Law*.[36] All these permissions remained exceptional. The ordinary minister of Confirmation remained the bishop, and he continued to exercise this ministry widely in his diocese for the benefit of those baptized earlier by priests and deacons.

> The children will receive the sacrament of baptism, the bishop or priest who baptizes them will also confer confirmation, and the children will for the first time participate in the liturgy of the eucharist.
>
> —*Rite of Christian Initiation of Adults*, 305

The RCIA brought to a head the twentieth-century developments permitting priests to confirm in certain circumstances. This restored an earlier sacramental practice in which the bishop administered the three initiation sacraments to candidates who had been prepared for them. The main difference is that the priest may perform a Confirmation formerly reserved to a bishop.

However, two historical developments soon found themselves in conflict: the restoration of the initiation sacraments to a single celebration and

---

33. Turner, *Ages of Initiation*, ch. 12, part 7.
34. *Code of Canon Law* (CIC), cc. 889 §2, 891.
35. RCIA, 14.
36. See CIC, cc. 883 2°, 885 §2.

the advancing minimum age for conferring Confirmation on those baptized in infancy. Parishes soon faced the dilemma that children younger than the diocesan age for Confirmation were being confirmed on the day of their Baptism. In the United States, the rebellion against the practice has been widespread. Even though the *Code of Canon Law* not only permits but obliges priests to confirm children of catechetical age whom they baptize, one survey shows that only 47 percent of them do.[37]

Nonetheless, the council's vision was clear-eyed, and its theology for the restoration of full initiation to children was sound.

Baptism

The initiation rites for children share the same paschal character as those for adults. As the *Rite of Baptism for Children* suggests the Easter Vigil or some Sunday as the most appropriate day for Baptism,[38] so the RCIA makes the same recommendation for children of catechetical age.[39]

The RCIA coined the term "catechetical age." In the past, vari-

The reforms of the Second Vatican Council restored the initiation sacraments to a single liturgy.

ous documents associated the "years of discretion" with the Sacraments of Penance and Confirmation, and the age of "the use of reason" for the first reception of Communion. Because the conferral of full initiation rites for children restored a practice that predates both of these expressions in Church history, the RCIA created another expression for its concerns.

The historical age for the conferral of Confirmation was linked to the age for the conferral of Penance because confession is encouraged prior to Confirmation and because both sacraments may be administered before first Communion. The appropriate age is called "of discretion" because of the history of Penance, which required one to be able to tell the difference between right and wrong in order to be found guilty of sin.

---

37. Turner, "MyRCIA: The Meaning of Adult Initiation in Post-Vatican II America," paulturner. org/wp-content/uploads/2014/10/MyRCIA-web-site.pdf, p. 7.

38. *Rite of Baptism for Children*, 9.

39. RCIA, 304.

The "age of reason" is for those who can tell the difference between ordinary food and drink and Eucharistic food and drink. "Catechetical age" obviously refers to the years when a child can learn. It predates the age for

the use of reason. The RCIA includes unbaptized children "who have attained the use of reason and are of catechetical age"[40]; however, in Latin the original edition refers not to those who have attained the use of reason but to those at the "age of discretion." The difference is slight, yet significant. The catechumenate is for children who are slightly younger than the age required for first Communion.

Children receive the initiation sacraments at the Easter Vigil because of the link between the rites and the Paschal Mystery.

The Easter Vigil and Sundays are the preferred occasions for the full initiation of children because of the link between these rites and the Paschal Mystery (the Passion Death and Resurrection of Christ).[41] Baptism produces its effects "by the power of the mystery of the Lord's passion and resurrection."[42] As St. Paul says, the baptized are united with Christ in his Death and Resurrection.[43] Baptism "recalls and makes present the paschal mystery itself, because in Baptism we pass from the death of sin into life."[44] This applies to children as well. Their sins forgiven, they step into new life with Christ.

Baptism fulfills the command of Christ, who asked his disciples to teach all nations and baptize them.[45] The Church's "most basic and necessary duty" is "to inspire all, catechumens, parents of children still to be baptized, and godparents" to true faith in Christ.[46]

Baptism incorporates people into the Church and builds them into a house where God lives.[47] It makes Christians a holy nation and a royal priesthood.[48] This unchangeable effect is expressed in the anointing with

40. RCIA, 252.
41. RCIA, 304.
42. *Christian Initiation*, General Introduction (CI), 6.
43. Romans 6:4 – 5.
44. CI, 6.
45. Matthew 28:19.
46. CI, 3.
47. Ephesians 2:22.
48. 1 Peter 2:9.

Chrism,[49] which accompanies the sacraments that can be received only once: Baptism, Confirmation, and Holy Orders. Baptism makes a person an adopted child of God, to use an expression that St. Paul favored,[50] and a sharer in God's own life.[51]

Baptism "washes away every stain of sin, both original and personal."[52] Yet because of its other effects it is superior to the purifications of the Old Law.[53] Even children experience all of this in the moment that they are baptized.

Confirmation

Few Catholics dispute the virtues of Baptism. Although there are some Catholic parents who lamentably neglect or avoid the Baptism of their children, the sacrament is still much requested. Its benefits are clear.

The Confirmation of young children is another matter. In recent decades the minimum age for previously baptized Confirmation candidates has increased and diversified in the United States. In neighboring dioceses the age of Confirmation for one may be seven, and for the other, sixteen. *The Order of Confirmation* envisions the possibility that the sacrament will be administered before or at the first Communion ceremony,[54] and some dioceses choose this option. But

The Order of Confirmation envisions that Confirmation could be part of the liturgy of first Communion.

they are few in number. It surprises many people, then, that an unbaptized child in the catechumenate may be confirmed at an age much younger than other children in the diocese.

---

49. CI, 4.
50. Romans 8:15; Galatians 4:5–6.
51. 2 Peter 1:4.
52. CI, 5.
53. CI, 6.
54. *The Order of Confirmation*, 13.

The most important explanations for confirming a newly baptized child of catechetical age are offered in the RCIA's commentary on the sacraments of initiation and in the *Code of Canon Law*. These explain the two most puzzling circumstances of this event: the age of the child and the choice of the minister. The RCIA's position is that Confirmation must follow Baptism immediately unless some serious reason interferes. It argues this with strong theological language:

> The conjunction of the two celebrations [of Baptism and Confirmation] signifies the unity of the paschal mystery, the close link between the mission of the Son and the outpouring of the Holy Spirit, and the connection between the two sacraments through which the Son and the Holy Spirit come with the Father to those who are baptized.[55]

Thus, it is not just that Baptism has a meaning and that Confirmation has a meaning, but that the conjunction of the two celebrations has yet another meaning. The conjunction signifies the unity of the Paschal Mystery. It shows

The Trinitarian nature of the sacraments of initiation is conveyed when the three sacraments are received at one liturgy.

that the gift of the Spirit (represented in Confirmation) fulfills the Son's mission (represented in Baptism). It represents the Trinitarian experience of the initiation rites. These are significant concepts, and to divide them obscures the central meaning of these sacraments.

Still, one may object, what does a child understand of these theological matters? Wouldn't a child benefit more by giving Confirmation catechesis later? The *Code of Canon Law* explains it this way: a priest has the faculty to confirm a child he baptizes (though not an infant),[56] and he must use this faculty for the sake of the child in whose favor the faculty was granted.[57] The reason the child is confirmed is *for the benefit of the child*. The child will receive the gift of the Holy Spirit as help throughout the rest of life. The child will experience full initiation, the full embrace of the Church's sacraments for those who seek incorpora-

55. RCIA, 215.
56. CIC, c. 885 §2.
57. CIC, c. 885 §2.

tion into the Body of Christ. They are sealed with the Spirit and made more ready for their participation in Holy Communion. If people believe in the power of the sacraments and the presence of the Holy Spirit, the benefits of an early Confirmation are clear.

Some people still object that confirming younger children is unfair to older children, which may stem from a sense of entitlement. However, the Church is so anxious to confer this gift of the Holy Spirit upon the child that priests receive the faculty to confirm those they baptize. This surprising choice of the minister represents a significant change to the practice in the Latin Rite Roman Catholic Church. But it is done for a pastoral reason: the benefit of the child.

> The sacrament of confirmation is to be conferred on the faithful at about the age of discretion, unless the Episcopal Conference has decided on a different age, or there is a danger of death.
>
> —*Code of Canon Law*, canon 891

Communion

Sharing in the Eucharist is the ultimate goal of the initiation of children. Like adults, they will now be able to participate more fully in the entire Liturgy of the Eucharist: the recitation of the Creed in which they were baptized; the Prayer of the Faithful, of whom they are now a part; the offering of the sacrifice of their lives in union with the sacrifice of Christ, of whose body they are now members; the praying of the Our Father as adopted children through Baptism; the sharing of the Sign of Peace as an initial symbol of Christian unity; and above all the sharing of Communion in the Risen Christ, who promised eternal life to those who ate his flesh and drank his blood.[58]

The Eucharist is the climax of the initiation sacraments because it incorporates one fully into the life of Christ.

The participation in the Eucharist is so significant that the RCIA's description of the celebration of the sacraments of initiation for children

---

58. John 6:54.

echoes the typical description for the opening of any Mass. Prior to the Second Vatican Council, the first words from the Missal's Order of Mass said that the ceremony would begin when the priest was ready (*Sacerdos paratus*). Now the opening of the Order of Mass says that the ceremony begins when the people have assembled (*Populo congregato*). The first words of the opening of the Mass of Christian initiation for children say that the ceremony begins when the children who are catechumens have gathered (*Congregato pueris catechumenis*) with their parents and godparents, neighbors and friends.[59] Subtly, this liturgy begins by indicating the way the children are expected to participate at every Mass in the future: gathered with others in the assembly.

During that Mass, after the conferral of Baptism and Confirmation, the children present themselves for Communion. The celebrant is to remind the children of "the preeminence of the eucharist, which is the climax of their initiation and the center of the whole Christian life," according to RCIA, 584. He may use his own words, but this final catechesis shows where their process of initiation has been leading. The children are soon to join the community at the common table, and to be united intimately with Christ their life. They will also find here the nourishment that will guide them all their days.

> If the Eucharist is truly the source and summit of the Church's life and mission, it follows that the process of Christian initiation must constantly be directed to the reception of this sacrament.
>
> —*Sacramentum caritatis*, 17

At first Communion, many parents hope that their child will believe in the Real Presence of Christ in the Eucharist and will receive the sacrament worthily. These are noble goals, but there is more. The Eucharist is the climax of Christian initiation because it incorporates one fully into the life of Christ, and it is the center of the future life of the child. The Church wants more than a first Communion. The Church wants weekly Communion. That will keep the child centered on the spiritual life.

Preparation

The very existence of a catechumenate for children demonstrates the Church's belief that the sacraments are not merely adult experiences. They can be shared with children. This implies a belief in God's grace at work in every

---

59. RCIA, 309.

human being. The practice of infant Baptism offers an extreme example of the Catholic Church's belief that God offers grace freely so that all may benefit from it abundantly.

After the Second Vatican Council, the Catholic Church made a wide liturgical outreach to children in order to put this belief into practice. Three Eucharistic Prayers for Masses with Children were added to those already available in the Missal. The *Directory for Masses with Children* gave generous provisions for adjusting the celebration of the Mass to engage children more earnestly. The *Rite of Penance* includes services directed for children. The *Rite of Pastoral Care and Anointing of the Sick* has prayers for a sick child. Even the Order of Christian Funerals contains special prayers for the death of a child.

> In the sacrament of the altar, the Lord meets us . . . and becomes our companion along the way.
>
> —*Sacramentum caritatis*, 2

This outreach extended into the initiation rites as well. The *Rite of Baptism for Children* was revised to face the reality that an infant could not understand the rite's words and actions. Changes to the ritual after the council affected the Ephphetha Rite, which previously had always come before Baptism in anticipation of speaking the baptismal promises for the first time. Now it is optional, and when it is used, it still precedes the Baptism of an adult, but it *follows* the Baptism of a child. It possesses a new purpose—to prepare the child for bearing witness to the faith later in life. In addition, some words formerly addressed to the child are now addressed to parents and godparents.

The postconciliar *Rite of Christian Initiation of Adults* includes a section on children of catechetical age. This is the most developed of all the revised liturgical ceremonies directed to the needs of a child. It demonstrates pastoral care but also a profound belief in the power of God's grace.

The RCIA foresees the possibility that unbaptized children may be preparing together with other children who are already baptized and still need to celebrate the Sacraments of Confirmation and Eucharist.[60] Unbaptized children will also require the assistance of adults, with as much support from parents as possible.[61] The RCIA thus envisions that the preparation of children takes place within a supportive community of their peers, parents,

---

60. RCIA, 254 §1.
61. RCIA, 254 §2.

guardians, and catechists. The initiation of children is not a private matter, but something that pertains to the entire Church.

These baptized companions, incidentally, lend another insight into the RCIA's theology of Confirmation. This section of the RCIA presumes that previously baptized children normally prepare for both Confirmation and first Communion around the same time. It suggests that such children are also preparing for their first confession.[62] It states that *unbaptized* children would celebrate their full initiation when *baptized* children are receiving Confirmation or Eucharist.[63]

> It must never be forgotten that the reception of Baptism and Confirmation is ordered to the Eucharist.
>
> *Sacramentum caritatis*, 17

If the bishop is not present for the celebration, he should grant the priest the faculty to confirm the children who were baptized as infants.[64] The celebrant should give attention to previously baptized children making their first Communion at the same celebration of full initiation.[65] All of this indicates that the people who prepared this section of the RCIA never envisioned a situation where the diocesan age of Confirmation for previously baptized children would differ very much from the age of first Communion. They focused so strongly on the unity of the three sacraments, that they did not foresee the pastoral dilemma.

Nonetheless, those preparing children for these three sacraments should only expect to offer formation appropriate to the age of the child. Some catechists fear that an eight-year-old preparing for full initiation has to have the same catechetical preparation as a high school student preparing for Confirmation. But this is not so. "The Christian initiation of these children requires both a conversion that is personal and somewhat developed, in proportion to their age, and the assistance of the education they need."[66] Some people have preconceived expectations of personal conversion for Baptism and sacramental preparation for Confirmation, but these should not determine the appropriate age of the candidate. It is the age of the child that determines the level of conversion and the content of the catechesis. Once again, the RCIA bases its treatment of children's initiation on God's invitation and grace.

---

62. RCIA, 293.
63. RCIA, 256.
64. RCIA, 308.
65. RCIA, 329.
66. RCIA, 253.

Conclusion

The English translation of the RCIA includes a feature that does not appear in the Latin original. It sets a scriptural allusion at the head of each prominent section. For example, in the section on adult initiation, the Period of the Catechumenate begins with a reference to Abraham: "Leave your country, and come into the land I will show you."[67] The Rite of Election or Enrollment of Names begins with a reference to the Book of Psalms: "Your ways, O Lord, are love and truth to those who keep your covenant."[68]

The section of the book treating Christian Initiation of Children Who Have Reached Catechetical Age cites a famous saying of Jesus: "Do not keep the children from me."[69] In the Gospel story, Jesus makes this remark because some of the disciples were trying to keep children away from him when parents were hoping he would bless the children and lay hands on them. The disciples were well-meaning but misguided.

Today we still find some people objecting to the full initiation of children. They think children are too young to understand the Eucharist, too inexperienced to prepare for Confirmation, too unworthy for Baptism.

Maybe. But maybe not.

The history of Christian initiation developed from a fundamental theology of the goodness of God. The Word of God took the form of an infant so that all human beings—even children—might share in divine life. The ministry of initiation is one way that the Catholic Church responds to Jesus' command: "Do not keep the children from me."

---

67. RCIA, 75, referring to Genesis 12:1.
68. RCIA, 118, referring to Psalm 25:10.
69. RCIA, 252, referring to Mark 10:14–15; Matthew 19:14–15; Luke 18:16–17.

The Rite of
Christian Initiation of Adults

Those who have received from God the gift of faith in Christ, through the
Church, should be admitted with liturgical rites to the catechumenate.

—*Ad gentes*, 14

The *Rite of Christian Initiation of Adults* (RCIA) is our era's guide to implementing the long and storied practice of Christian initiation, which arose from the charge the Lord Jesus gave his disciples: "Go, therefore, and make disciples of all nations, baptizing them in the name of the Father, and of the Son, and of the holy Spirit, and teaching them to observe all that I have commanded you."[1] Every age has responded to this charge in a way that reflects the culture and needs of the Church in that day. We are no different.

The RCIA is an official rite of the Roman Catholic Church that carries the same weight in the Church as the other sacramental rites. It provides a process of periods and steps through which not only adults but also children of catechetical age are initiated into the Church.

Each person who comes to the parish seeking a deeper relationship with God through the Church has a story and a call from God. The Christian initiation process allows them to know God through the Church and the Scriptures as they move gradually through periods that are marked by liturgical rites.

In the first period of the process, the Period of Evangelization and Precatechumenate, *inquirers* come to know God as they hear the Scriptures and become acquainted with members of the Church. As they listen to the Scriptures, they ponder how their own stories intersect with the story of Christ. Opening their hearts to God, they see how he has been part of their lives in their joys and in their struggles, always seeking relationship. During this time of inquiry, they begin to learn how to pray, and as they come to know God's love for them, they start to develop a desire to change their lives.

---

1. Matthew 28:19–20.

When the inquirers are ready, the parish community formally welcomes them with a liturgical rite as they declare their intent to become members of the Church. With this Rite of Acceptance into the Order of Catechumens, these inquirers become *catechumens* and begin the Period of the Catechumenate.

During this period the catechumens are apprenticed in the Christian way of life as it is lived in the Catholic Church. As they prepare to celebrate the Sacraments of Baptism, Confirmation, and Eucharist, they participate in the Liturgy of the Word at Sunday Mass, from which they are dismissed after the homily to continue to reflect on God's Word. They participate in catechesis that acquaints them with teachings and traditions of

> The catechumenate . . . is not merely an exposition of dogmatic truths and norms of morality, but a period of formation in the entire christian life.
>
> —*Ad gentes,* 14

the Church and instills in them a sense of the mystery of salvation. They learn to turn to God in prayer, to ponder the Word of God, and to hope in God in their daily lives. As they form relationships in the parish, they begin to participate in apostolic works. During this time, the Church strengthens the catechumens through Celebrations of the Word, Blessings, and Anointings.

After the catechumens, with the help of members of the Christian community, have discerned readiness to receive the sacraments of initiation, they join catechumens from throughout the diocese and stand before the bishop at the Rite of Election at the beginning of Lent. At this liturgy, the bishop hears the testimony of those who know the catechumens. And, having done so, he declares them the elect and states that they will be initiated at the Easter Vigil. The catechumens are now called the *elect* and enter the Period of Purification and Enlightenment.

The Period of Purification and Enlightenment ordinarily takes place during Lent. This period is more retreat-like than catechetical, in preparation for the celebration of the Easter sacraments. On the Third, Fourth, and Fifth Sundays of Lent, the liturgical rite called the *Scrutinies* are celebrated with the elect during Mass. As part of this rite, the assembly prays that what is weak or sinful in the hearts of the elect will be uncovered and healed, and what is strong will be strengthened. At other liturgies within this period, the elect are presented with the Creed and the Lord's Prayer to prepare them to take their place among the baptized.

Children of catechetical age are baptized at the Easter Vigil after journeying through the periods of the Rite of Christian Initiation of Adults.

At the Easter Vigil, after hearing the Scripture stories of the creation and salvation of the world, the elect take their place in that story through the Sacraments of Baptism, Confirmation, and Eucharist. During the Period of Mystagogy that follows, the newly baptized, now called *neophytes*, will reflect on the sacraments they have received and on the mysteries of faith in light of those sacraments.

Children and the *Rite of Christian Initiation of Adults*

The periods and rites described in the *Rite of Christian Initiation of Adults* apply to children of catechetical age just as they do to adults. Children of catechetical age who seek the initiation sacraments also, will follow a path that includes the periods that are marked by liturgical rites. Their journey through the initiation process also will be gradual and will include times of discernment with their parent and sponsor, as well as a priest, catechist, or other member of the initiation team. During the Period of the Precatechumenate, those who minister with the child discern whether he or she has begun to call on God in prayer, feel sorrow for wrongdoing, and have a sense of the Church. Before children move from the Period of the Catechumenate to the Period of Purification and Enlightenment, they will have shown a spirit of faith and charity, a sufficient acquaintance with Church teaching, and an intention to receive the sacraments. At the Easter Vigil, the assembly will rejoice with the children as they are baptized, confirmed, and welcomed to the Eucharistic table.

Part I of the RCIA, titled "Christian Initiation of Adults," deals with the evangelization and formation of unbaptized, uncatechized adults and the rites that are appropriate to them as they make the journey from inquiring about the Christian faith and the Catholic Church to full initiation through the Sacraments of Baptism, Confirmation, and Eucharist and beyond.

Part II, chapter 1, of the RCIA concerns the Christian initiation of children of catechetical age. These unbaptized children are considered adults under Church law for most situations, but their religious and developmental needs are different from those who have reached the age of majority. This chapter offers ways of adapting Part I of the RCIA for children while keeping its vision and pattern. At times, this book will refer to Part I for the clarity it provides in directives regarding a rite.

> The Christian initiation of these children requires both a conversion that is personal and somewhat developed, in proportion to their age, and the assistance of the education they need.
>
> —Rite of Christian Initiation of Adults, 253

This book is for those who minister to these children. Within these pages, Christian initiation ministers will be supported in celebrating the rites in their fullness with children of catechetical age.

Periods and Steps in the Rite of Christian Initiation of Adults

	First Period	First Step	Second Period
	Period of Evangelization and Precatechumenate	Rite of Acceptance into the Order of Catechumens	Period of the Catechumenate
Time	Indefinite length	When inquirer and community discern readiness	At least a year year (including Period of Purification and Enlightenment)
Name	**Inquirer**		**Catechumen**
What occurs during this period or step	Proclamation of the Gospel and Jesus Christ, leading to faith and initial conversion; introduction to the Christian community	Inquirers publicly declare their intention to become members of the Church; Church accepts them as catechumens.	Formation through catechesis, experience of the Christian way of life through familiarity with community, participation in the liturgical life of the community, and participation in the apostolic life of the Church
Rites belonging to the period	No formal rites; individual prayers and blessings may take place as appropriate.		Celebrations of the Word, Blessings, Anointings, Minor Exorcisms

Second Step	Third Period	Third Step	Fourth Period
Rite of Election	Period of Purification and Enlightenment	Celebration of Sacraments of Initiation	Period of Mystagogy
First Sunday of Lent	Lent	Easter Vigil	Easter Time; extended Mystagogy for one year
	Elect		**Neophyte**
In the name of the Church, the bishop judges readiness of catechumens for initiation and declares that they are chosen for sacraments at the next Easter Vigil.	Retreat-like preparation for the celebration of sacraments of initiation	Initiation into the Church through Baptism, Confirmation, and Eucharist	Deepening understanding of Paschal Mystery though meditation on the Gospel, participation in the Eucharist, and doing works of charity
	Scrutinies, Presentations of the Creed and Lord's Prayer, Preparatory Rites on Holy Saturday		Sunday Masses of Easter Time; celebrations near Pentecost and anniversary of initiation; Mass with the bishop

Preparing the Rite of Acceptance into the Order of Catechumens

Let the children come to me; do not prevent them,
for the kingdom of God belongs to such as these.

—Mark 10:14

Period of Evangelization and Precatechumenate

The initiation process formally begins with the celebration of the Rite of Acceptance into the Order of Catechumens. During this rite, the children will state their desire to become a member of the Body of Christ and their intention to receive the sacraments. The rite ritualizes the movement from observing and questioning to publicly declaring and being recognized as preparing for the sacraments of initiation. The children move from outside to inside, from strangers to members of the household. Their presence among us is the fruit of our lives as Christians, bringing Christ to the world in the witness of our lives and in the work of evangelization.

Before the Rite of Acceptance, though, the child takes part in the important Period of Evangelization and Precatechumenate. This period is flexible; it does not correspond with a particular liturgical season and has no set length or end date. It can be considered a season of a person's life during which he or she responds in a formal way to God's invitation to enter into a relationship of faith. During this time, God touches the child's heart and draws him or her to seek to know him through Jesus Christ.

This may occur in many ways. Most often an unbaptized child comes to the Church for initiation because of a family situation. Perhaps the parents are Catholics who stopped practicing their faith and never had their children baptized in infancy but now desire that the family become active members. A parent coming to faith for the first time might bring her children with her; or a member of the parish might adopt an older child who was never baptized. Sometimes, though, a child may seek Baptism on his own. He may feel drawn to do so because he knows a Christian family whose generosity and kindness touches him. Or she may attend a Catholic school and respond to the teachings and values she finds there. However it happens, being drawn to the Church is a sign of God at work in the children's lives, inviting them to know and love him.

During the Period of Evangelization and Precatechumenate, the Christian community is charged with evangelizing the child who has responded to God's invitation. This child often is referred to as an *inquirer*.

> Faithfully and constantly the living God is proclaimed and Jesus Christ whom he has sent for the salvation of all. Thus those who are not yet Christians, their hearts opened by the Holy Spirit, may believe and be freely converted to the Lord and commit themselves sincerely to him. For he who is the way, the truth, and the life fulfills all their spiritual expectations, indeed infinitely surpasses them.[1]

The purpose of evangelization is to make known the living God, especially as he is revealed through Jesus Christ. Two primary ways individuals of any age come to know Christ are the Scriptures and the Church.

During this period, both the Old and the New Testaments must be shared in a way that shows that God has always cared for people and all of creation, and still does today. Children may have heard Bible stories or seen cartoon versions of them, but it is important that they become familiar with the stories as a way of knowing who God is and why Jesus came among us.

Children also become acquainted with Christ through the Church. During this period, it is especially important that these youngsters come to know Christ through those who know him through faith. These include the saints to whom we look for inspiration and the living members of our church communities, especially other children who can model what it means to believe and live as a Christian. The stories that these children tell of their faith and relationship with Christ will help the young inquirers come to know the Lord.

> From evangelization, completed with the help of God, come the faith and initial conversion that cause a person to feel called away from sin and drawn into the mystery of God's love.
>
> —*Rite of Christian Initiation of Adults*, 37

Usually, children have many questions about the Church during this time; hearing and understanding the answers help build their relationship

---

1. RCIA, 36.

with the Church. The questions may be simple or challenging. The children may inquire about the meaning of a particular symbol or image, or they may want to discuss something they heard about the Church in the news or from a family member. They may wonder why Catholics do some particular thing or why bad things happen. Questions should be answered in a way appropriate to the child's ability to understand, and in a way that is more than simply factual. For example, a question about a certain image may prompt a story of a saint, or invite the child to look at other images for clues about the person portrayed. If an answer to a question is not known, the person queried should admit lack of knowledge and ask for time to research the answer. Questions also may be more personal, requiring individual conversation with a priest or other trained minister, or a counselor.

Another important element of building relations with the Church is getting to know members of the Christian community socially. Children and their families should know they are welcome to attend parish-wide events. Certainly, children should be introduced to other parish children, who could serve as companions along their journeys. Catechumenal families might be introduced to other families who are at similar stages in life. Connecting a catechumenal family to a sponsor family may be helpful at this point. Sponsor families share their faith in informal settings and introduce members of the

Children and families should be encouraged to attend parish events to get to know others in the parish.

catechumenal family to others. People just coming to the Church may be testing whether there is a way for them to fit into parish life. The bonds of friendship and shared interests often help sustain us in faith.

Like all relationships, the relationship with God in Christ is strengthened and deepened through communication. Children should be encouraged to begin to pray if they have not already done so. Discussing the reasons for prayer—blessing and adoration, petition, intercession, and thanksgiving—and the customary times for prayer may help them understand how prayer fits into their lives.

There are no formal prayers or rituals prescribed for this period, but clergy, catechists, and sponsors should begin and end their time with the children with prayer. Blessings provided in the rite for the Period of the Catechumenate[2] may be appropriate.[3]

The purpose of evangelization is that the children may come to know Christ so that they can enter a relationship with him and be converted to him. Conversion is the heart of the process of Christian initiation. The Period of Evangelization and Precatechumenate must be conducted in such a way that the child's relationship with God, which began at God's initiative, is fostered and deepened.

> Blessings are signs that have God's word as their basis and that are celebrated from motives of faith.
>
> —*Book of Blessings*, 10

Discerning Children's Readiness for the Rite of Acceptance into the Order of Catechumens

Before the Rite of Acceptance into the Order of Catechumens is celebrated, readiness for this step needs to be discerned. The child does this with the Church, represented by the clergy, catechists, sponsors, and others.[4]

The *Rite of Christian Initiation of Adults* provides guidance and tells us what to look for as we discern children's readiness to celebrate the rite. Although the chapter "Christian Initiation of Children Who Have Reached Catechetical Age," in Part II, gives us guidelines and rubrics for celebrating the rite with children,[5] we must refer to Part I for a description of what to look for as we determine if a child is ready to move to the Period of the Catechumenate. Let's consider a real-life scenario.

St. Benedict Parish scheduled a celebration of the Rite of Acceptance into the Order of Catechumens for the beginning of November. Delaney and Nicholas have been participating in inquiry with their mother, Kelly, since September. All three of them went to St. Benedict's intergenerational initiation sessions and the children went to some religious-education classes, but their attendance was sporadic. Delaney and Nicholas were with their dad every other weekend, and that had a big effect on their level of participation.

---

2. RCIA, 95–97.
3. RCIA, 40.
4. RCIA, 43.
5. RCIA, 260–276.

Do we just assume that since they have been in the precatechumenate period for two months, they are ready to become catechumens and enter the Period of the Catechumenate?

Paragraph 42 of the rite tells us that there must be evidence of an initial conversion. It also states that we should look for

- an intention to change their lives and to enter into a relationship with God in Christ;
- evidence of the first stirrings of repentance;
- a start to the practice of calling upon God in prayer;
- a sense of Church;
- Some experience of the company and spirit of Christians through contact with a priest or with members of the community.

This may seem like a lot to ask of children, but these requirements can be adapted in a developmentally appropriate way. For example, "evidence of the first stirring of repentance" for children means that they recognize when they have done wrong and that they show signs of sorrow for the wrongdoing. Notice that all of the prerequisites given in paragraph 42 are beginnings. "A start," "evidence," "a sense," "some experience" direct us to look for initial signs of conversion in the children.

We can look in one other place before determining if a child is ready to celebrate the Rite of Acceptance: the rite itself. The rite tells us a great deal about the expectations the Church has of the children who come to it.

The opening dialogue between the celebrant and the children as it is given in paragraph 264 tells us quite a bit:

Celebrant: "What do you want to become?"
Children: "A Christian."
Celebrant: "Why do you want to become a Christian?"
Children: "Because I believe in Christ."
Celebrant: "What do you gain by believing in Christ?"
Children: "Eternal life."

This dialogue, which is a model for an actual dialogue, indicates that the children must have some understanding of what it means to be a Christian and what it means to join a Christian community. Furthermore, if the rite is to be celebrated well, the children must also know what it means to believe in the Christ who gives them eternal life. That is a lot to ask for some children.

They do not necessarily understand the meaning of Christ and eternal life by being in a precatechumenate for two months.

After the dialogue, the rite continues with the signing of the candidates with the cross.[6] During this action, the children are covered with the Sign of the Cross. This part of the rite tells us that the children need to have some perception of the power and the meaning of the cross before they are covered with the sign of our salvation. A prayerful reading of the entire rite[7] gives further clues as to what the Church expects of her young catechumens.

Understanding the rites is a precursor to discernment for the rites. Discernment is a serious, yet enjoyable and personal process that facilitates conversations among children, parents, sponsors, and pastoral ministers.

Step One: Talk to the Parent

The first step in discerning the child's readiness is to explain the significance of the ritual moment to the parent or guardian. This explanation can be given to a group or during a one-on-one conversation. It is helpful for parents to recognize that the rite marks the transition from the first period of formation to the second period of formation, and that their children are being officially accepted by the Church as catechumens. It may be helpful to give the parent a guide with a few questions to be discussed with the child. (See Step Two.)

In addition, the parents are asked to reflect upon their faith journey, especially if they are also candidates for initiation. Whether or not the parents are candidates or Roman Catholic, they are involved with their child in this journey of conversion; therefore, the discernment questions are directed to the parents as well as the children.

Step Two: Parent (and Sponsor) Talks to the Child

The discussion that takes place between a parent and child is relaxed. It is not a formal question-and-answer dialogue but a conversation between parents and children. If the sponsor is standing in for the parent, or if the sponsor is helping the entire family, the sponsor may want to share in the dialogue. This conversation may happen informally at home, in the car, or anywhere. The time for this conversation also could be incorporated into an inquiry session.

---

6. RCIA, 266–268.
7. RCIA, 260–276.

The conversation starters that follow will help the parent and/or the sponsor see how initial conversion is taking place in the child, in the parent, and in the family. Many of the discussion points are based on paragraph 42 of RCIA, and the Rite of Acceptance for children, paragraphs 260–276.

- Tell me what you like about the parish (or Church).

- What are some of things you've learned about God? Jesus? The Holy Spirit?

- What are some Bible stories you like?

- Tell me about how you pray.

- What do you think it means to be a follower of Jesus? Why do you want to be a follower of Jesus? Do you need to change anything in your life to be a better disciple?

- What about Jesus' Cross? What does the Cross mean to you?

- What would you like to ask God? How can God help you?

- What would you like to ask the Church? How can the Church help you?

Step Three: Respond and Decide

After the parent and child have had an opportunity to reflect upon the child's readiness for the Rite of Acceptance, they should discuss their responses with the initiation coordinator, a catechist, a sponsor or the sponsor family, or a priest.[8] This discussion to determine the child's readiness can be an informal conversation or it could be incorporated into a day of reflection and discernment. Some parishes schedule "Discernment Days" as part of their overall initiation process. The RCIA does not tell us exactly how to do discernment, but we are advised in paragraph 43 that "sufficient and necessary time, as required by each case, should be set aside to evaluate" before the Rite of Acceptance is celebrated. As the Rite clearly directs, the Rite of Acceptance may be celebrated two or three times a year.[9] This means there is no rush for children to celebrate this ritual. Let's return to Delaney and Nicholas and their mother, Kelly, as an example of celebrating the rite when the children are ready.

Following the steps outlined earlier, Kelly talked with the RCIA coordinator and her children about celebrating the Rite of Acceptance. Delaney and Nicholas did not have much to say when Mom talked with them about

---

8. RCIA, 43.
9. RCIA, 18.

Jesus and the Church. Although they had attended a handful of sessions, they had not yet developed an understanding of what it means to be a follower of Jesus Christ. As she talked with her children, Kelly saw that, too. She realized that the whole family, herself included, needed more time to develop the sense of what it means to a Christian.[10]

Thus, Kelly and her children continued in the precatechumenate period. They attended RCIA family sessions and came to church more regularly. St. Benedict's paired them with a sponsoring family and they got to know other families in the parish. Then, that spring they celebrated the Rite of Acceptance into the Order of Catechumens and began the Period of the Catechumenate.

> God showers his grace on the candidates, since the celebration manifests their desire publicly and marks their reception and first consecration by the Church.
>
> —*Rite of Christian Initiation of Adults*, 41

Preparation for the Rite of Acceptance into the Order of Catechumens

The Rite of Acceptance may be celebrated at any time of the year. Although it is not prohibited, most parishes avoid the Sundays of Lent and Advent. The rite presumes that the catechumenate will be "an extended period."[11] The bishops of the United States have directed that this period "should extend for at least one year."[12] The date for the celebration of the Rite of Acceptance should be selected accordingly.

It may be helpful for pastors or other initiation ministers to reserve two or three dates as possible times to celebrate this rite.[13] These dates may be selected for the appropriateness of the prescribed Scripture readings and their availability on the parish calendar. If there are children ready to become catechumens as a reserved date draws near, scheduling is done; if not, the reservation can be removed from the calendar.

The Rite of Acceptance may take place within or outside Mass. But wherever it occurs, the rite should be prepared so that it is an integral part of the liturgy and should be celebrated with the same care and preparation that characterize the rest of the parish's liturgical life. Those preparing the rite will

---

10. RCIA, 42, 264.
11. RCIA, 75.
12. *National Statutes for the Catechumenate* (NS), 6.
13. RCIA, 18.

recognize how it differs from most of the sacramental celebrations and blessings that occur at Mass. Most rites takes place after the Word of God is proclaimed and preached. The Rite of Acceptance, however, is literally an entrance rite during which the children ask to be admitted into the household of faith and the assembled Church welcomes them in. It replaces the usual Introductory Rites of the Mass, just as does the Reception of the Children when infant Baptism is celebrated at Mass. The Penitential Act and the Gloria do not take place when the Rite of Acceptance is part of the liturgy.

The director of the catechumenal process should work with the celebrant, the liturgy director, and the music director to prepare this liturgy. It may be helpful to begin preparing this and the other rites of the initiation process long before the date of the Rite of Acceptance so that the way that the rites are celebrated in a given year and over a longer period of time might be cohesive. The outline of the rite will help in visualizing the steps and sequence.

Rite of Acceptance into the Order of Catechumens

Receiving the Children

- Greeeting
- Opening Dialogue
- Affirmation by the Parents (Sponsors) and Assembly
- Signing of the Candidates with the Cross
  - Signing of the Forehead
  - Signing of the Other Senses (Optional)
- Invitation to the Word of God

Liturgy of the Word

- Instruction
- Readings
- Homily
- Presentation of a Bible (Optional)
- Intercessions for the Children
- Prayer over the Children
- Dismissal

The Place and Context for Celebration

In many parishes, the children participate in the Rite of Acceptance with adults. However, whether the children will be part of the same rite as the adults and where the rite will take place is decided in the parish. The chapter "Christian Initiation of Children Who Have Reached Catechetical Age" recommends in paragraphs RCIA, 257 and 260, that the rite need not occur with the whole parish. Paragraph 257 states, "For children of this age, at the rites during the process of initiation, it is generally preferable not to have the whole parish community present, but simply represented." Paragraph 260 notes in regard to the Rite of Acceptance that "it is important that this rite be celebrated with an actively participating but small congregation, since the presence of a large group might make the children uncomfortable."

These recommendations seem to contradict Part I of the RCIA, which repeatedly indicates the importance of the presence of the community at the rites of the catechumenal process. In particular, RCIA, 9, enumerates the ways that the faithful support the candidates and catechumens:

The entire community must help the candidates and the catechumens throughout the process of initiation: . . . At the celebrations belonging to the period of the catechumenate, the faithful should seek to be present whenever possible and should take an active part in the responses, prayers, singing, and acclamations. . . . The faithful should take care to participate in the rites of the scrutinies and presentations.

At most parishes in the United States, the rites of the initiation process for children are celebrated at the parish Sunday Mass, often in combination with adults in the process.

The chapter on the initiation of children is sensitive to the needs of children that are different from adults in the catechumenal process. Paragraphs 257 and 260 are great examples of that concern. But the final pastoral decision rests with those who know the children and the parish best. In the United States, it seems that most parishes celebrate the rites of the initiation process at the parish Sunday liturgy, often in combination with adults in the same process, especially when family members are seeking initiation at the same

The director of the catechumenal process, the celebrant, and liturgy and music directors may want to prepare the liturgies for each of the rites of the initiation process long before the Rite of Acceptance is celebrated.

time. The descriptions of the liturgies given in this book will assume that this is primarily the case.

Parishes should assess the real situation of the children they are ministering to as they make their decisions.

Ministers of the Liturgy

When the Rite of Acceptance into the Order of Catechumens is celebrated within Mass, a priest presides; a priest or deacon may preside if it is celebrated outside Mass.[14] If possible, the celebrant should already be acquainted with the children, their parents, and their sponsors.

A full complement of ministers—readers, cantor and other musicians, servers—should be present at this liturgy; it is an important occasion in the life of the Church and in the relationship between the Lord and those who are to become catechumens. If the liturgy is not part of a regular parish Mass or not during Mass, appropriate ministers will still be needed, especially readers and musicians. All ministers should be informed that the liturgy will be somewhat different from the usual and prepared to take their part in it.

Parents, sponsors, and companions also have an active part in this rite, and they should be prepared for it. The parents and sponsors should be given an explanation of what will be expected of them and, if possible, walked through the rite. If they will be signing the children with the Sign of the Cross, they should be shown how to do so. The Sign of the Cross is made by actually touching the child with the fingertips, with the hand open. The signing is done gently, but with enough pressure that the impression of the cross may be felt and remembered.

As paragraph 42 of the rite notes, the inquirers should also be instructed about the rite. They should be prepared to answer the questions that will be asked of them and given a general understanding of how the rite will progress, but they should not have to worry about where they need to be and when. The parents, sponsors, and other ministers of the rite should lead them through it.

---

14. RCIA, 45.

Ushers and ministers of hospitality could alert parishioners as they enter that something special is occurring at this liturgy. If worship aids have been prepared for this rite, they should be sure everyone has one. These ministers can also help with the movement in and out of the church by making sure that doors are open and there are no obstacles in the way.

The children who are serving as companions to the child catechumens may be invited to sit with them after they enter the church for the Liturgy of the Word.

With so many people involved in a rite with a lot of movement, it may be helpful to have someone unobtrusively shepherd the various participants through the liturgy. A liturgy coordinator, master of ceremonies, adult server, or the initiation director might undertake the task.

Ministers of hospitality can distribute participation aids and alert people that the Rite of Acceptance into the Order of Catechumens will occur at the Mass.

Music for the Rite

Some hymnals have music for the rites of initiation, and most of the Catholic liturgical music publishers have collections for this purpose; appropriate music that is already part of the parish's repertoire might also be used. The Christian initiation coordinator should discuss the musical requirements of the various parts of the rite with the music director and ask that person to help with the selection of music.

At several places in the Rite of Acceptance, acclamations are prescribed and in other places, they may be appropriate. Many parishes find that using the same set of acclamations whenever this rite is celebrated helps the assembly participate more fully and interiorize the words. A brief rehearsal with the congregation to teach or review an acclamation is especially valuable the first few times this rite is celebrated.

In addition, there are processions to be accompanied by music. The movement from outside the church to inside should be accompanied. The rite recommends certain psalms as options; the proper Entrance Antiphon or other Entrance Song of the day may be appropriate. The departure of the catechumens after they are dismissed also requires processional music. A refrain that echoes the celebrant's words of dismissal in the adult rite, "Catechumens, go in peace, and may the Lord remain with you," might be appropriate. It may also be appropriate to repeat the antiphon of the Responsorial Psalm.

Liturgical Environment

The Rite of Acceptance requires little of the liturgical environment. The place where the initial gathering takes place might be made a bit more festive than usual with banners or greenery. The church should be decorated appropriately for the time of the liturgical year. There are a number of times in this rite when people move and stand in various places. Care should be taken that nothing obstructs these movements or the sightlines of the assembly.

Preparing the Assembly

The Rite of Acceptance, like the entire initiation process, belongs to the whole parish. For the assembly to celebrate it fully, consciously, and actively, they will need to understand what this rite is, who the inquirers are, and what the symbols of the rite mean. They also need assistance in understanding what this rite means for them. Help them connect to the signing of the senses by evoking the many times they as Catholics sign themselves or are signed. Most especially recall when they signed their children or godchildren at their Baptisms, and make the connection between that ritual moment in the Baptism of children and the signing at the Rite of Acceptance, because they are the same rite. Brief explanations and questions for reflection could appear the weekend before the rite is celebrated and again on the weekend it is celebrated in the bulletin and other means the parish uses to communicate. Pictures of the new catechumens could be included, if the parents agree.

Prepare the assembly for the signing of the catechumens by relating it to the signing that occurred at Baptism.

Celebrating the Rite of Acceptance into the Order of Catechumens

Receiving the Candidates

To symbolize that the children are moving from outside the Church to inside, the rite ideally begins outside the church. At least a representative portion of the assembly should be able to be accommodated in the space. A plaza in front of the church, a large narthex or gathering space, a hall, or other large room would be appropriate. If no such space is available, it may take place just inside the church doors.[15]

The movement from outside the church proper to entering the church for the Liturgy of the Word is a powerful sign of what it means to be accepted as a catechumen. However, it may not always be possible for the rite to occur outside, especially if the assembly for the rite is large, as it often is when celebrated at a Sunday Mass. Wherever the rite begins, preparers of the liturgy must consider how the assembly will participate. The congregation should be able to see, to hear, and to respond in word and song.

The congregation should be able to see, hear, and respond in word and song to the actions during the Rite of Acceptance.

The rite begins when the celebrant greets the children, who have gathered at the appointed place outside the church (or inside the doors of the church) with their parents and sponsors and other members of the faithful.[16] If the assembly consists of more than those who are gathered with the inquirers, the celebrant could begin in the church and invite those inside to accompany him to greet them; if the rite will take place at the back of the church, he or another minister may invite the assembly to turn to the back of the church. As the celebrant walks toward the inquirers, a psalm or appropriate song may be sung.

The celebrant's greeting to the children is to be simple and friendly, expressing the Church's joy at their presence. Unlike the rite for adults, in the text of the rite adapted for children, the celebrant does not ask the inquirer his or her name. In some parishes, the celebrant just speaks to the child by

---

15. RCIA, 48.
16. RCIA, 48.

The Rite of Acceptance could begin in the church with those inside accompanying the celebrant to meet the inquirers.

name. (If there are a number of children, name tags are helpful.) But since this rite provides an opportunity for the assembly to get to know the children, it would be valuable for the parent, sponsor, or companion to introduce the child.

After the greeting, depending on the placement of the celebrant in relation to the children, they and their parents, companions, and sponsors may move forward to stand in front of him.

The celebrant then asks each child about their intentions in coming to the Church. The text provides questions that the celebrant may ask, but there is great flexibility in how he queries the children.[17] Prior to the rite, the children should be prepared for these questions about why they have come to the Church; it may be helpful for their catechists, parents, or sponsors to help them consider their answers beforehand. After the dialogue with the children, the celebrant speaks to them briefly about what it means to be a catechumen,[18] ending this short catechesis by asking the children for a sign of their assent. That sign may be given by the children's repeating his last words, "Love God with all your heart and love one another as I have loved you," or the children could respond in a way that is similar to the dialogue with adults.

Affirmation by the Parents (Sponsors) and the Assembly

The celebrant asks the parents (or sponsors who are standing in their place) if they give their consent to have the child prepared for Baptism. (If the parents are not present for this rite, it is important that the parents give their assent to the priest or catechist before the rite is celebrated.) He then asks if they will take part in the children's preparation. Finally, he asks the whole assembly if they are ready to help.

---

17. RCIA, 264.
18. RCIA, 264, offers an example.

Signing of the Candidates with the Cross

If the place where the children, parents, companions, sponsors, ministers, and assembly have gathered does not allow everyone to see the signing of the candidates, many parishes move into the church at this point, especially if the signing of the senses will be included. Psalm 63:1–8, or a reprise of what was sung as the celebrant approached the inquirers might appropriately accompany this movement.

The rite envisions that the signing will take place where the earlier parts of the ritual have taken place, so do so if it is possible. It will help emphasize the symbolism of the catechumens' entrance into the church to hear the Word of God at the end of the rite.

The celebrant invites the children and their parents, companions, and sponsors forward for the signing.[19] If this is to be done inside the church, and everyone has just entered the church from outside, wait until all are seated and settled. In that case, it may also be better for the children and their parents or sponsors to wait in the back of the church until they are called forward.

The signing is a powerful symbol for the whole assembly. When preparing this liturgy, consider where the children and parents or sponsors will stand for the signings. Depending on the size and configuration of the church, the children may be placed across the front of the church, facing the assembly; they might also be placed in the aisles, some near the front of the church, some closer to the back, so that all the members of the assembly can see this important action.

The celebrant speaks the given formula for the signing of the forehead once, then signs each child on the forehead in silence. If that is to be the only signing, the celebrant may invite the parents (if baptized), sponsors, companions, or the catechist also to sign the children on the forehead.[20]

The signing of the inquirers on the forehead and, often, on all the senses is an important aspect of this rite. In the preparation of this rite, it is important to be aware that the signing is done by actually touching the forehead and other parts of the body. Paragraph 266 suggests that the signing of the other senses after the forehead may be more appropriate for "somewhat older" children. This should be discussed with the children, parents, and sponsors

---

19. RCIA, 54, 268.
20. RCIA, 267.

beforehand. If there are any for whom this is inappropriate for cultural or other reasons, adaptations are to be made.[21]

If the senses are also to be signed, the celebrant may do all the signings, saying the formula for each of the signings for each child.[22] Alternatively, the celebrant may speak the formula for each sense as the parent, sponsor, companion, or catechist does the signing.

Whether there is one signing or many, an acclamation is sung after each one. The rite suggests "Glory and praise to you, Lord Jesus Christ," for which

most parishes will already have a musical setting, since it is one of the Lenten Gospel acclamations. Another appropriate acclamation may be used.

The signing concludes with the celebrant making the Sign of the Cross over the candidates, individually or all at once, while saying, "I (we) place you entirely under the sign of Christ's cross in the name of the Father, and of the Son, and of the Holy Spirit: live with Jesus now and for ever." The children reply, "Amen."

The signing concludes with the celebrant making the Sign of the Cross over the candidates.

Invitation to the Word of God

The celebrant invites the catechumens and their parents, companions, or sponsors to the Liturgy of the Word. If they and the rest of the assembly are still outside the church, the movement into the church should be a procession, possibly led by ministers with cross and candles, and certainly accompanied by singing. The rite suggests Psalm 95 or 122; the rite for adults suggests Psalm 34 with the antiphon, "Come, my children, and listen to me; I will teach you the fear of the Lord." Another suitable song may also be chosen. If everyone is already in the church, the celebrant may invite the catechumens to take their place in the assembly, either with their parents or sponsors or with the children who are serving as their companions.

---

21. RCIA, 33 §3, 54.
22. RCIA, 268.

Liturgy of the Word

The celebrant briefly addresses the catechumens and the whole assembly to help them understand the importance of the Word of God proclaimed.[23] The readings are proclaimed in the usual manner, with a sung Responsorial Psalm and Gospel Acclamation, whether or not the rite is part of the celebration of the Eucharist.

Readings

If the rite is celebrated at a Sunday Mass or other Mass where the readings are obligatory, the readings prescribed for that Mass are proclaimed. If the rite takes place outside of Eucharist or at a Mass other than a Sunday Mass, the rite suggests that the readings may be taken from those given in the *Lectionary for Mass* at number 751, Christian Initiation apart from the Easter Vigil,[24] or at number 743, Entrance into the Order of Catechumens, under Ritual Masses, I. For the Conferral of Christian Initiation: Genesis 12:1–4a, Responsorial Psalm 33:4–5, 12–13, 18–19, 20 and 22.[25] Any other suitable readings from the Lectionary also may be proclaimed.[26] A homily on the readings is preached, followed by a time of silence.

Presentation of a Bible

After a time of silence, the rite directs that a suitable song is to be sung that may be accompanied or followed by the giving of a Bible to each child. The children may be called forward so that a Bible (or a book containing the Gospels) may be presented to them by the celebrant or a catechist. If this is done, the homilist may have explained the meaning of the giving of a Bible, or some words of explanation may be given at this point. In the rite for adults, the words of presentation are "Receive the Gospel of Jesus Christ, the Son of God."[27] If the Rite of Acceptance takes place at Mass, the song might be omitted and an acclamation sung following this action. This presentation of a Bible is optional; the Bible could also be presented at a separate Celebration of the Word or in a catechetical session.

---

23. RCIA, 61, 270.
24. RCIA, 271.
25. RCIA, 271.
26. RCIA, 25, 271.
27. RCIA, 64.

Intercessions for the Children

The assembly then prays for the new catechumens. The children may be invited to stand facing the assembly as these prayers are prayed, if they are not already in that position. These are prayers of intercession, similar in structure to the Universal Prayer (Prayer of the Faithful), but specific in nature. A response different from that customarily used at Mass may emphasize the difference. Because intercessory prayer is the duty of the baptized, the catechumens are silent during this prayer.

If the rite is being celebrated at Mass, the usual prayers of intercession, the Universal Prayer, may be prayed after the children are dismissed, or they may be omitted. In that case, intentions for the Church and the world are added to the intercessions for the catechumens.[28]

Prayer over the Children

A prayer spoken by the celebrant with hands outstretched over the children concludes the intercessions and the Rite of Acceptance.

———————●●●━━━━━━━━━━

From this time on the Church embraces the catechumens as its own with a mother's love and concern. Joined to the Church, the catechumens are now part of the household of Christ, since the Church nourishes them with the word of God and sustains them by means of liturgical celebrations.

—*Rite of Christian Initiation of Adults*, 47

Dismissal

If the Rite of Acceptance has been celebrated outside Mass, everyone is dismissed at this point.[29] If the Liturgy of the Eucharist is to follow, the catechumens are normally dismissed to continue reflecting on the Word of God. The children and their catechist may be invited forward before the words of dismissal are spoken. They should have their coats and other belongings with them. The celebrant expresses the great joy of the rite just celebrated and dismisses the children with words of peace. A suggested formula is given in RCIA, paragraph 276; two others are found in paragraph 67A, B. Music, preferably a refrain sung by the whole assembly may accompany the procession. The sponsors remain until the end of Mass and may join the

---

28. RCIA, 65, 68.
29. RCIA, 276.

catechumens at that time. If the parents are also catechumens, they may be dismissed at the same time.

If for some reason the children cannot be dismissed, they are invited to remain and are gently reminded that they must await the day of their Baptism before they may participate fully at the Lord's table. A sample formula for this situation is provided at paragraph 67C. Catechumens are never dismissed simply to go home at this point.

The dismissal should take place at every Eucharistic liturgy the catechumens attend until they are initiated, so this dismissal sets the pattern for the others. It should be noted, though, that this dismissal occurs after the Intercessions for the Children and that at most liturgies, that dismissal takes place before the Creed, and thus before the Universal Prayer.

The dismissal provides an opportunity to catechize the faithful about the meaning of their Baptism and of the responsibilities of the baptized, who have put on Christ. In intercessory prayer, the faithful take on the priestly role of Christ to intercede with the Father for the needs of the world. In the Eucharistic Prayer, the faithful participate in Christ's eternal prayer of thanks and praise to the Father; in Holy Communion, they receive the Lord to whom they have been eternally joined; at the dismissal they are sent out to live the Gospel in word and deed. This is what the children who are now catechumens are preparing for. The rest of the members of the assembly should be reminded of the dignity that is theirs and rejoice with those who are preparing to share in that dignity.

Liturgy of the Eucharist

If the Eucharist follows, the Universal Prayer may be prayed. It could be introduced as a continuation of the Intercessions for the Catechumens (for example, Let us continue to pray for the needs of the Church and the world) or it could be introduced in the usual way. As mentioned earlier, the Universal Prayer may be omitted. In addition, the Profession of Faith may be omitted[30] and the Eucharist continues with the Preparation of the Altar and the Gifts. These permissions recognize that the Rite of Acceptance may take a bit more time than the ordinary Introductory Rites and allows the rite to be celebrated in an unhurried manner.

---

30. RCIA, 67.

Preparing the Rites Belonging to the Period of the Catechumenate

Whoever receives one child such as this in my name, receives me;
and whoever receives me, receives not me but the One who sent me.

—Mark 9:37

The Minor Rites

The rites belonging to the Period of the Catechumenate are often referred to as the "minor rites" to distinguish them from the rites that mark the movement from one period to another. The word *minor* in this case is not meant to communicate that they are unimportant or optional. Catholics believe that God the Father, through Christ and in the Spirit, is present and active among us in our rites and liturgies. These minor rites are among the means by which God moves among us and acts on us, shaping us and forming us in the journey of conversion.

In Part I of the *Rite of Christian Initiation of Adults*[1] six minor rites that belong to the Period of the Catechumenate are presented for use with adults:

- Celebrations of the Word of God
- Minor Exorcisms
- Blessings of the Catechumens
- Anointing of the Catechumens
- Presentations of the Creed and the Lord's Prayer
- Rite of Sending to the Cathedral for Election by the Bishop

Of these minor rites, the chapter "Christian Initiation of Children Who Have Reached Catechetical Age" specifically mentions only the Presentations. This does not mean that the other rites are not to be used. Rather, those preparing children for initiation should consider what is helpful for the children they are ministering to and how best to adapt the rites to their needs.

---

1. RCIA, 81–117.

Celebrations of the Word of God

"Among the rites belonging to the catechumenate, then, celebrations of the word of God are foremost."[2] There is an importance attached here to these celebrations. They are foremost both in terms of their necessity and their frequency. A Celebration of the Word is most appropriate at every catechetical session during the catechumenate, especially at the beginning of the session. If sessions are being held at the same time for adults and children, the groups could begin together with a Celebration of the Word and then separate for catechesis.

Other gatherings of the catechumens would also present a good opportunity to celebrate the Word of God. If the children and their parents or sponsors are taking part in a parish service activity, for example, a simple Celebration of the Word might set the service in a scriptural context. A priest, deacon, or a qualified catechist or other lay minister may preside at Celebrations of the Word.

Elaborating on the Celebrations of the Word of God, the RCIA notes, "During the period of the catechumenate there should be celebrations of the word of God that accord with the liturgical season and that contribute to the instruction of the catechumens and the needs of the community."[3]

Celebrations of the Word are never celebrated outside the context of the time of the liturgical year in which they occur. This is important because, as noted in the *Universal Norms on the Liturgical Year and the General Roman Calendar* (UNLY), the document that gives provisions for the liturgical year, "Over the course of the year the Church celebrates the whole mystery of Christ, from the Incarnation to Pentecost Day and the days of waiting for the Advent of the Lord."[4]

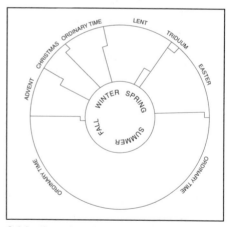

Celebrations of the Word are celebrated within the context of the liturgical year in which they occur.

These Celebrations of the Word help to facilitate the process of conversion and formation; they contribute to the instruction and catechesis that the

---

2. RCIA, 79.
3. RCIA, 81.
4. UNLY, 17.

children receive. Paragraph 82 presents four purposes of Celebrations of the Word:

- to implant in [the catechumens'] hearts the teachings they are receiving: for example, the morality characteristic of the New Testament, the forgiving of injuries and insults, a sense of sin and repentance, and the duties Christians must carry out in the world;
- to give them instruction and experience in the different aspects and ways of prayer;
- to explain to them the signs, celebrations, and seasons of the liturgy; and
- to prepare them gradually to enter the worship assembly of the entire community.

The term *Celebrations of the Word* can refer to a well-proclaimed passage from Scripture, surrounded by the singing of a song and a psalm, using the familiar greetings, introductions, and conclusions. It can also mean a more solemn ritual, more closely resembling the Liturgy of the Word at Sunday Mass. It can happen in a variety of settings, with a small number of people or a large assembly.

The rite provides the following structure for the Celebration of the Word of God:[5]

Celebration of the Word of God

- Song
- Readings and Responsorial Psalms
- Homily
- Concluding Rites

This model is quite sparse; it does not indicate all the usual elements of the Liturgy of the Word at Mass. Because one purpose of these Celebrations is to prepare the catechumens to enter the assembly, it is appropriate to include these elements.

The catechist may determine the degree of solemnity of the celebration. If the celebration will be in the room where catechesis will take place, candles and a cross can be placed near where the reading will occur to provide a reverent atmosphere. A chapel or church setting might call for a bit more ceremony.

---

5. RCIA, 85–89.

An opening song may be sung while all, including the celebrant, are standing in their places or while the celebrant (and perhaps others) process in. The music might take the form of a simple, appropriate song the children already know or one that they can learn for a season. A catechist or member of the parish music ministry might accompany the hymn or lead the song without accompaniment.

The celebrant leads the Sign of the Cross and greets those gathered. A penitential act may take place, as at Mass, followed by a Collect (opening prayer).

The reading(s) and Responsorial Psalm would be chosen from Scripture for their relevance to the formation of the catechumens and proclaimed by one of the members of the initiation ministry, a sponsor, companion, or another baptized person.[6] These readings should be chosen carefully, depending on the occasion. If the gathering is for the weekly catechetical session, then the readings and psalms should reflect the topics of catechesis for that session. If the occasion is to take part in the community soup kitchen, for example, then the readings and psalms might focus on service or on how the Lord feeds and cares for us.

Of course, the number and length of the readings depends on the children's ages and ability to understand. These readings should be proclaimed with all of the formularies that are familiar to a Liturgy of the Word: "A reading from . . ." to begin the proclamation, and "The Word of the Lord / Thanks be to God" to conclude it. This helps familiarize the children with these liturgical phrases and how they are used.

If the parish is using a particular hymn or Responsorial Psalm for a season, that might be used if appropriate with the chosen readings.

While technically a homily is reserved to the deacon or priest, as with other rites of the Church (for example, Blessings from the *Book of Blessings,* or rites from the *Pastoral Care of the Sick*), lay leaders may give a brief explanation of the readings. This brief explanation might help to situate the catechesis or other activity within the context of prayer.

The Celebration of the Word may end simply, with the customary liturgical conclusion of a blessing. If an ordained minister is leading, it would be the ordinary "May almighty God bless you . . . ." If a lay minister is leading, then it would be the blessing used by a lay minister, "May almighty God bless

---

6. RCIA, 87.

us, protect us from all evil, and bring us to everlasting life," said while making the Sign of the Cross.

However, as RCIA, 89, states, "the celebration of the word may conclude with a minor exorcism (94) or with a blessing of the catechumens (97). When the minor exorcism is used, it may be followed by one of the blessings (97) or, on occasion, by the rite of anointing (102–103)." (These other rites will be examined individually in the following section.)

The rite concludes with a blessing. If appropriate, a song may be sung.

Minor Exorcisms

Catechists and other ministers who work with children on the journey of Christian initiation should understand the purpose of the Minor Exorcisms and make a pastoral judgment about the appropriateness of using them.

The Minor Exorcisms of the catechumenate are signs of the redemptive mission of Christ, who came to save us from all that threatens to keep us from him and all that threatens us as his disciples. There is much in life today that threatens to keep us from Christ: sin, selfishness, greed, the pursuit of power and prestige, a disregard for the poorest and weakest among us.

The RCIA contains the texts of the various prayers of exorcism.[7] Their themes and composition, such as hesitation in faith, love of money, hatred, quarreling, greed, lust, and pride, are certainly more appropriate for adults than for children. But in the lives of children, fear, uncertainty, anger, and difficult situations at home or school also can be barriers to developing faith in Christ.

When such concerns arise with the children, simple prayers similar to the exorcisms for adults may be added to the regular Celebration of the Word of God, before the final blessing; at the conclusion of a catechetical session; or even prayed privately for an individual child, with the parent or sponsor. Notice that these prayers not only name the concern, but ask God for something: protection, peace, open hearts, endurance. Such prayers teach children (and adults) that they can always turn to God in difficulty and that God will be with them and help them.

In the Minor Exorcism, the catechumens bow their heads or kneel before the celebrant and the celebrants prays over them. The children respond, "Amen."

---

7. RCIA, 94.

Minor Exorcism

- Prayers of Exorcism
- Catechumen bows head or kneels before celebrant (priest, deacon, or qualified catechist).
- Celebrant, with hands outstretched, prays the text of one of the ten prayers provided (A–K), or an appropriate adaptation.
- Catechumen responds, "Amen."

Blessings of the Catechumens

The blessings of the catechumens are a sign of God's love and of the Church's tender care. They are bestowed on the catechumens so that, even though they do not as yet have the grace of the sacraments, they may still receive from the Church courage, joy, and peace as they proceed along the difficult journey they have begun.[8]

As with the Word of God, blessings are meant to stir in us remembrance of all the good that God has bestowed upon us throughout history. This stirring of memory prompts us to ask in faith for more. Blessings, then, are an act of faith—an act of faith for the Church and an act of faith for the catechumens.

As with the exorcisms, those who minister to the children in the catechumenate should determine how the Blessings of the Catechumens may best be used. Also like the exorcisms, the blessings provided in Part I of the RCIA are better suited to adults than children. They are, however, good models of what such blessings do for the children: they ask God to form, bless, sanctify, teach, strengthen, lead, and help them. These prayers could be shortened and put in simpler language for use with children. The children could even learn to recognize what they want to request from God, which could be incorporated into prayers of blessing.

> Whether God blessed the people himself or through the ministry of those who acted in his name, his blessing was always a promise of divine help, a proclamation of his favor, a reassurance of his faithfulness.
>
> —*Book of Blessings*, 6

---

8. RCIA, 95.

Celebrations of the Word of God would be a most opportune time to celebrate a Blessing of the Catechumens; they could also conclude a catechetical session or an individual conversation with a child.

Blessings are given by a priest, a deacon, or, as with the Minor Exorcisms, by a qualified and trained catechist who has been appointed by the bishop. When in a group, the minister extends hands over all the children together and prays the blessing aloud. If possible and appropriate, he or she then lays hands on each child in silence.

Blessing of the Catechumens

- Prayer of Blessing
- Celebrant (priest, deacon, qualified catechist) has outstretched hands over the catechumens.
- Celebrant says one of five blessings, 97A—I.
- Celebrant extends hands over all the children and, if appropriate, lays hands on them individually.

Anointing of the Catechumens

The words used in the Anointing of the Catechumens are the same as those in the anointing with the Oil of Catechumens in the *Rite of Baptism for Children*: "We anoint you with the oil of salvation in the name of Christ our Savior; may he strengthen you with his power, who lives and reigns for ever and ever. Amen." The prayer, whether for an adult, a child, or an infant, symbolizes the need for Christ's help to resist evil so that the individual may come to profess Christ and remain faithful to him.

Preceding the anointing is a prayer of exorcism that requests that the catechumens be strengthened in the face of whatever threatens to keep them from Christ. The single exorcism prayer given for the Anointing of Catechumens is drawn from the account in Luke when Jesus enters the synagogue in Nazareth and reads from the scroll of the prophet Isaiah: "The Spirit of the Lord is upon me, because he has anointed me to bring glad tidings to the poor."[9] However, any of the Prayers of Exorcism given in paragraph 94 may be used.

The Anointing of the Catechumens takes place primarily as part of the conclusion to a Celebration of the Word of God but may be conferred privately

---

9. Luke 4:18.

for pastoral reasons.[10] These Anointings can take place several times during the course of the catechumenate,[11] whenever it might seem beneficial to the catechumens. The celebrant is a priest or deacon.[12]

If the oil to be used is not that which was blessed by the bishop at the Chrism Mass, a priest, for pastoral reasons, may bless oil immediately for the anointing. In this case, this prayer of blessing replaces the initial exorcism. A deacon cannot bless the oil.[13]

The minister then prays the Prayer of Anointing once over all the cate-chumens, who answer, "Amen." The minister then goes to each catechumen and anoints him or her on the breast or on both hands. Traditionally, anoint-ing the catechumens on the breast was a sign of the protection the anointing gives them, a visual allusion to armor, or a breastplate. That allusion can be lost today, since such protection is no longer worn. For that reason, and particularly with children, anointing both hands might be the better pastoral choice.

The anointing might be given, "if this seems desirable, even on other parts of the body."[14] In some parishes, the forehead is anointed. Since the neophytes will be anointed on the forehead with Chrism during their Confirmation at the Easter Vigil, anointing the hands might still be the better choice.

After the children are anointed, one of the options for the Blessing of Catechumens (or an adaptation) may be prayed over them. If this takes place within a Celebration of the Word of God, it would be followed by the final blessing of all who have gathered. The anointing could also take place after the homily at the celebration of Mass, at the same time as adult catechu-mens, if there are any.

> The anointing with oil symbolizes their (the catechumens') need for God's help and strength so that . . . . they will forthrightly take the step of professing their faith and will hold fast to it unfalteringly throughout their lives.
>
> —*Rite of Christian Initiation of Adults*, 99

Anointing of the Catechumens

- Prayer of Exorcism or Blessing of Oil

- If the celebrant (priest or deacon) is using blessed oil, prayer 102A is used. If the celebrant is a priest, he may bless oil oil for the anointing using prayer 102B.

---

10. RCIA, 100.
11. RCIA, 100.
12. RCIA, 98.
13. RCIA, 101.
14. RCIA, 103.

- Anointing

- The celebrant faces the catechumens and says the words of anointing.

- Catechumen responds, "Amen."

- The celebrant anoints each catechumen.

- The anointing may be followed by a blessing.

Presentations of the Lord's Prayer and the Creed

Though the *Rite of Christian Initiation of Adults* allows for these rites to be anticipated in the Period of the Catechumenate, it also notes that they "normally take place during Lent."[15] For this reason, they will be treated in this book when the rites of the Period of Purification and Enlightenment are addressed.

Preparing for the Rite of Sending Catechumens for Election

Even though the Rite of Election or Enrollment of Names is presented as optional,[16] initiation ministers should consider the importance of this rite. The rite is the second step toward the initiation sacraments and begins the Period of Purifications and Enlightenment. Still, ministers will need to decide with the parents or sponsors if the children will participate in the diocesan celebration of the Rite of Election. If it is decided that the children will be part of the Rite of Election, the parish may decide to include the youth in the Rite of Sending the Catechumens for Election, but this too is an optional rite, and it is particular to the Church in the United States. (The rite is also optional for adults.)

The Catholic bishops of the United States approved this rite because the majority of the parish community will not go to the cathedral for the Rite of Election. For this reason, the Rite of Sending the Catechumens for Election closely resembles the Rite of Election and gives the "local community the opportunity to express its approval of the catechumens and to send them forth to the celebration of election assured of the parish's care and support."[17]

---

15. RCIA, 104.
16. RCIA, 277.
17. RCIA, 107.

In reality this rite is a wonderfully pastoral adaptation by the bishops of the United States.

The election of the catechumens is, the Rite reminds us, the "focal point of the Church's concern for the catechumens."[18] For this reason, the opportunity for the parish to express its judgment as to the progress and the readiness of the catechumens is important.

Before exploring the Rite of Sending the Catechumens for Election, we will consider the discernment process for the Rite of Election.

Discerning Readiness for the Rite of Election

In the same way the Rite of Acceptance marks the beginning of the Period of the Catechumenate, the Rite of Election "marks the beginning of the period of final preparation for the sacraments of initiation, during which the children will be encouraged to follow Christ with greater generosity."[19] The final period of preparation, the Period of Purification and Enlightenment, "usually coincides with the beginning of Lent" and is "celebrated with children of catechetical age, especially those whose catechumenate has extended over a long period of time."[20]

Likewise, the discernment process is similar to the process used prior to the Rite of Acceptance, but in this case the Church looks for deeper conversion and readiness for the sacraments.[21] Indeed, the Church is specific about judging the children's readiness for the sacraments. RCIA, 278, notes:

> In the rite of election, on the basis of the testimony of parents, godparents and catechists and of the children's reaffirmation of their intention, the Church judges their state of readiness and decides on their advancement toward the sacraments of initiation. Thus the Church makes its "election," that is, the choice and admission of those children who have the dispositions that make them fit to take part, at the next major celebration, in the sacraments of initiation.

Involving the parents is very important at this stage, as it has been throughout the entire process of initiation. The children's godparents are specifically mentioned for the first time, and their involvement along with

---

18. RCIA, 107.
19. RCIA, 277.
20. RCIA, 277.
21. RCIA, 119, 120.

the parents and catechists is also important. But now the Church is asking for a judgment of the children's "dispositions" for the sacraments.

For a clearer understanding of what the Church means by "dispositions that make them fit to take part . . . in the sacraments of initiation," we return to Part I of the rite. Paragraph 120 gives guidance regarding what is expected of a catechumen before she or he celebrates the Rite of Election. Of course, these criteria are adapted for children:

- a conversion in mind and in action;
- a sufficient acquaintance with Church teaching;
- a spirit of faith and charity;
- deliberate will and enlightened faith; and
- an intention to receive the sacraments.

The Rite of Election for children gives us further suggestions about what happens before the children celebrate election. The questions asked of the children in paragraph 283 give an indication that the Church expects that the children have

- a desire for Baptism, Confirmation, and Eucharist;
- listened to the word of God;
- lived like Jesus' followers; and
- taken part in the community's life of prayer and service.

To illustrate how the discernment process plays out in real life, let's return to the story of Delaney and Nicholas and their mom, Kelly. Remember that the children and their mom became catechumens in the spring. By the following winter, it appeared that they were ready to enter the Period of Purification and Enlightenment on the First Sunday of Lent. Thus, several weeks prior to Lent, the discernment process began.

The process used for discernment was similar to that used in discerning readiness for the Rite of Acceptance. The three-step process was employed in a slightly different fashion.

Step One: Talk to the Parent

Kelly and her children had been in the catechumenate for months, so the initiation team and the parish knew them well. They had been participating in Sunday dismissal, going to catechetical sessions, and helping with the

Saturday pancake breakfasts for the hungry. They had participated in the first Communion retreat, and generally had been involved in parish life. It was easy for the coordinator to talk with Kelly and ask her if she thought the children were ready.

Yes, she thought they were. And, here are some of the reasons she gave:

- They want to come to church. They get up on their own and are ready before me!

- We pray at mealtime and at bedtime, too. We never used to do that.

- Delaney quit hanging around some of the mean girls. She acts differently now.

- Both of them talk about how they can't wait to be baptized.

- Nicholas says his best friend is Jesus.

Step Two: Parent and Sponsor Talk to the Child

Kelly felt strongly that her children were ready for the sacraments, but it's important for the children themselves to express the desire to receive the sacraments. During one of the family initiation sessions, Kelly and her parish sponsor talked with Delaney and Nicholas about their readiness to be baptized. The conversation included the following discussion points, based on the criteria given in paragraphs 120 and 283.

- Why do you want to be baptized and confirmed? What does it mean to you?

- Why do you want to receive the Eucharist? What does it mean to you?

- Tell me about how you talk to God.

- Tell me about your friendship with Jesus.

- What are some of your favorite Bible stories?

- How do you follow Jesus in your everyday life?

- What do you like about our parish?

- How has preparing for the sacraments made a difference in your life?

- What will you do differently after you are baptized?

- How will you live as a disciple of Jesus?

- What difference will it make that you are baptized and follow Jesus?

Step Three: Respond and Decide

After talking with the children and sharing their responses with the coordinator, it was clear Delaney and Nicholas were ready for the Rite of Election and the sacraments of initiation. Together, Kelly and her children participated in the preparation session for the Rite of Sending and Rite of Election and joined in the celebration of the Rite of Sending. Then they were on the way to the cathedral and the Period of Purification and Enlightenment.

Preparing the Rite of Sending Catechumens for Election

Day and Place the Rite Occurs

The Rite of Sending may take place at a Celebration of the Word of God[22] with adults, but it is most commonly celebrated at Sunday Mass on the First Sunday of Lent or whichever day that the catechumens will go to the diocesan Rite of Election. When it occurs during Mass, the local parish community is able to take a particular part in the process of the catechumens being elected for full initiation. Many parishes that celebrate the Rite of Sending do so with adults and children at the same liturgy. Alternatively, it can be celebrated with a smaller community of family, sponsors, godparents, and others in the church or a smaller chapel or other room in the parish that is appropriately arranged. Those who minister with the children in the catechumenate will need to discern how it is most appropriate for them to celebrate this rite.

> This rite [the Rite of Sending the Catechumens for Election] offers that local community the opportunity to express its approval of the catechumens and to send them forth to the celebration of election assured of the parish's care and support.
>
> —*Rite of Christian Initiation of Adults*, 107

Scripture Readings

When the Rite of Sending is celebrated on the First Sunday of Lent, the Scripture readings are those of the day. If it is celebrated on another day, the readings of that day are used. If they are not appropriate, the readings of the First Sunday of Lent or other suitable readings should be selected.[23]

---

22. RCIA, 109.
23. *Lectionary for Mass*, 744.

Music

Little additional music for the Rite of Sending is called for if it is celebrated at a Sunday liturgy. If there are a large number of catechumens to sign the Book of the Elect, it may be appropriate for the assembly to sing a refrain or acclamation that expresses the weight of what is occurring at this moment. If such an acclamation or refrain was used during the Rite of Acceptance into the Order of Catechumens, consider repeating it here so that a thread is created between the rites.

If the rite is celebrated at a time other than a Sunday liturgy, music ministers and readers should be assigned to the celebration. This would be done as a more festive Celebration of the Word, with the singing of appropriate seasonal hymns and acclamations.

The Book of the Elect

The signing of the Book of the Elect is a profound yet simple moment. Like many of our liturgical symbols, such as breaking bread or pouring water, it takes an everyday action as a symbol of profound meaning. The ordinary act of signing one's name becomes a sign of the desire to enter fully into the life of the Church through the Easter sacraments.[24]

Depending on the practice in the diocese, the book may be signed during the Rite of Sending and presented to the bishop at the Rite of Election or signed at the cathedral as part of the Rite of Election. RCIA, 113, notes that the catechumens may sign the Book of the Elect after the Rite of Sending if there is an extraordinary number of catechumens.

The book itself should be substantial and well made, decorated appropriately but not ostentatiously. The same book should be used for both the children and the adults who are being sent for election. Over the years the book becomes a reminder of the journeys of faith of those who have been elected, part of the faith story of the community and the larger Church.

Consider where the signing of the book will take place. It may be held by an initiation minister as the catechumen signs, or it may be placed on a small table or podium, simply decorated. The signing should not take place on the altar.

---

24. RCIA, 132

Celebrating the Rite of Sending for Election

Homily

A homily is to be given by the celebrant. If this is a celebration for the children alone and the celebrant "finds it difficult in the homily to adapt himself to the mentality of children, one of the adults, for example, the children's catechist, may speak to the children after the gospel."[25] If this is a rite for both adults and children, the celebrant should address both groups in a way that the children can understand.

Presentation of the Catechumens

After the homily, an appropriate minister, such as the coordinator of initiation ministry, presents the children to be sent for election to the celebrant. The Rite of Election for children provides a formula,[26] noting that they have completed their preparation and that they have the support of the community. This presentation may be adapted and personalized according to the specific circumstances of the children.

The celebrant then calls the children to come forward with their parents and with those who will be their godparents. He or the minister who presented them should call them forward by name. They come forward, standing before the minister. Consider having the catechumens stand facing the assembly, perhaps on a step, with their godparents and parents behind, so that the whole assembly can see them. The celebrant could stand at the head of the aisle and face the catechumens when addressing them and then turn to the assembly. The exact placement will depend on the configuration of the church or other place and the number of catechumens to be sent for election, but keep in mind that the assembly should be able to look at the front of the catechumens.

Affirmation by the Godparents [and the Assembly]

The celebrant addresses all the parents, godparents, and the assembly, asking for their recommendation of the children. He then asks whether the children have "listened well to the word of God, . . . tried to live as his faithful followers, . . . [and] taken part in this community's life of prayer and service."[27] The language of these questions can be adapted, but the purpose

---

25. RCIA, 281.
26. RCIA, 282.
27. RCIA, 283.

should not change: to determine whether sufficient conversion has taken place for Baptism, according to the child's age and ability.

The celebrant may turn back to the people and ask for their approval of the catechumens. Companions may be encouraged to speak on the child catechumen's behalf. This affirmation by the assembly can be a powerful way for the people of the parish to claim their responsibility in the progress of formation and conversion of the catechumens.

The celebrant then turns to the children and declares that their parents, godparents, and the whole community has spoken well of them, and now they must say themselves that they want to follow Christ. He asks whether they "wish to enter fully into the life of the Church through the sacraments of baptism, confirmation, and the eucharist,"[28] to which they respond affirmatively. The Book of the Elect may be signed at this point.

Intercessions for the Catechumens and Prayer over the Catechumens

The whole assembly then prays for the catechumens in the intercessions. Paragraph 287 offers texts that can be used in the intercessions; these texts may be personalized or otherwise adapted. The intercessions conclude with the Prayer over the Catechumens, which the celebrant prays with hands outstretched over the catechumens. The prayer in paragraph 288A is appropriate.

The intercessions prayed by the assembly can be personalized to the catechumens.

If the Eucharist is to follow, the catechumens are dismissed in the usual manner. If not, all are dismissed.

If the Eucharist is to follow, the usual general intercessions in the Universal Prayer may follow, or they may be omitted, in which case, the intercessions for the Church and the world would have been included in the intercessions for the catechumens. The Mass would then continue with the Creed, although for pastoral reasons, it too may be omitted. The Preparation of the Altar and the Gifts follows as usual.[29]

---

28. RCIA, 284.
29. RCIA, 117, 289.

Preparing the Rites Belonging to the Period of Purification and Enlightenment

Let us come into his presence with thanksgiving;
let us make a joyful noise to him with songs of praise.

—Psalm 95:2

The Period of Purification and Enlightenment

The Period of Purification and Enlightenment is the time of final preparation for those who have been chosen for the Easter sacraments. This period, which customarily coincides with Lent, is a time of spiritual preparation, and is more retreat-like than catechetical. The preparation is largely liturgical.

> This period [Purification and Enlightenment] . . . is intended to purify the minds and hearts of the elect as they search their own consciences and do penance.
>
> —*Rite of Christian Initiation of Adults*, 139

The Scrutinies are rites of self-searching and repentance and they have, above all, a spiritual purpose: "to uncover, then heal all that is weak, defective, or sinful in the hearts of the elect; to bring out, then strengthen all that is upright, strong, and good."[1] They help the elect prepare to renounce sin and evil and profess faith in God at their Baptism. These are rites of purification in which the Church asks for strength for the elect as they enter into the final preparation for Baptism, Confirmation, and Eucharist. Through these rites, the elect gradually learn about the mystery of sin and increase their desire to be delivered from it.

The Presentations prepare the children to take their place among the baptized and to keep the faith they profess and their relationship to God as adopted children through Baptism always in their hearts and on their lips.

---

1. RCIA, 141.

Penitential Rite (Scrutiny)

Particular questions arise with the Penitential Rite (Scrutiny) presented in Part II, chapter 1, for children.[2] Initiation ministers often wonder why only one Penitential Rite (Scrutiny) is given when three are provided for adults. Further confusion occurs because the rite suggests that "these penitential rites are a proper occasion for baptized children of the catechetical group to celebrate the sacrament of penance for the first time."[3]

All this can seem very confusing and difficult to execute when examining this rite for the first time. A closer reading of the ritual text can eliminate the problem. The rites note that the children's progress in formation depends on the support that they receive from their companions as well as from their parents. Including baptized children of the catechetical group in the worshipping assembly is a way to be faithful to the vision of the rite, which sees the initiation of unbaptized children as taking place "within the supportive setting" of their baptized peers.[4]

> Because the penitential rites normally belong to the period of final preparation for baptism, the condition for their celebration is that the children are approaching the maturity of faith and understanding requisite for baptism.
>
> —*Rite of Christian Initiation of Adults*, 292

The very first paragraph describing the Scrutinies with children, advises that "the guidelines given for the adult rite (141–146) may be followed and adapted, since the children's penitential rites have a similar purpose."[5] A good principle to follow whenever questions arise regarding the rites for children is this: when in doubt, follow Part I.

Paragraph 294 makes a similar point; it notes that when celebrating a second Scrutiny with children, "the texts for the intercessions and prayer of exorcism given in the adult rite (153–154, 167–168, 174–175) are used, with requisite modifications." Overall, it is advisable to use the Scrutinies in Part I with unbaptized children, particularly when adults are also celebrating the Scrutinies. It is not necessary to celebrate separate Scrutinies with children.

In each particular case, however, initiation ministers should determine what is appropriate for the children to whom they are ministering, but the rite

---

2. RCIA, 291–303.
3. RCIA, 293.
4. RCIA, 254.
5. RCIA, 291.

is clear that at least one Scrutiny is to be celebrated. The issues to be determined are how many Scrutinies the children should celebrate, and whether those will be celebrated with adults, and where and when the Scrutinies will occur.

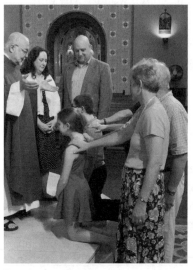

Parents, as well as the sponsors, accompany the children during the rites.

Still remaining is the question of baptized children receiving the Sacrament of Penance during the children's Scrutiny. Again, we turn to the adult rite for an answer. For adults, there is no Scrutiny or Penitential Rite in which the unbaptized and baptized are combined; paragraph 463 directs that combining the baptized with the unbaptized for Scrutinies and Penitential Rites is not to occur. Since the prayers of the Scrutiny refer to the elect's coming Baptism and the rite includes a prebaptismal exorcism, the baptized are not included in this rite. In carrying out these rites, one never wants to confuse what is appropriate for the unbaptized with what is appropriate for the baptized.

Combining a children's Scrutiny with the celebration of the first reception of Penance is joining two related but essentially different rites, one for the unbaptized and one for the baptized. Many initiation ministers who have celebrated the two together find it disconcerting and confusing.

We believe in you, Lord Jesus Christ. Fill our hearts with your radiance and make us the children of light!

—*Rite of Christian Initiation of Adults*, 597

It is an excellent practice, however, to have baptized children of the catechetical group present for the Penitential Rite (Scrutiny) with their unbaptized companions, but they should attend as members of the worshipping assembly. Attending the Mass with the Scrutiny is a good way to help them prepare for the Sacrament of Penance at another time, whether they are celebrating it for the first time or a subsequent time.

Preparation for the Scrutinies

This section on preparation will include information from both the adult rite, which may be adapted for celebration with adults and children or even with children alone, and the rite for children. The preference is for the adult rite, which seems more cohesive, but those who plan these Scrutinies will need to decide what is more appropriate for the children and community they minister to.

When

The three Scrutinies are celebrated on the Third, Fourth, and Fifth Sundays of Lent, at Sunday Mass.[6] For pastoral reasons they may be celebrated on other Lenten Sundays or even during the week. If one or two Scrutinies will be celebrated with the children only, they may be celebrated on Lenten Sundays or weekdays, at Mass or at Celebrations of the Word, approximately a week apart.

In the rare and unusual circumstance of the Period of Purification and Enlightenment taking place outside Lent, the three Scrutinies are celebrated on Sundays or even weekdays, with a week between them.[7]

Scripture

The readings for the Scrutinies that are celebrated with adults and which may include the children are always those of the Third, Fourth, and Fifth Sundays of Lent for Year A. The very heart of the rites of Scrutiny is the proclamation of the three readings from the Gospel according to John: the woman at the well (4:5–42) on the Third Sunday, the man born blind (9:1–41) on the Fourth Sunday, and the raising of Lazarus (11:1–45) on the Fifth Sunday. The use of these Gospel accounts in the preparation of those to be baptized dates to the fourth and fifth centuries. In their proclamation they illumine the lives of the elect. The narrative of these Gospels reveals how the elect need the life-giving water of Christ and the light of Christ that they may see the truth and the new life to which Christ calls them.

The Penitential Rites (Scrutinies) for children provide additional readings that may be used when the rites are celebrated only with children.[8] Those

---

6. See RCIA, 150–156, 164–170, 171–177.
7. RCIA, 146.
8. RCIA, 297.

are Ezekiel 36:25–28, Isaiah 1:16–18, Mark 1:1–5, 14–15, Mark 2:1–12, Luke 15:1-7, and 1 John 1:8–22.

Mass Texts

The prayers of the Mass for the three Scrutinies, found in the *The Roman Missal* under Ritual Masses: 2. For the Celebration of the Scrutinies, are used whenever they are celebrated at Mass.[9] The first of these includes a commemoration of the godparents and a proper form of the *Hanc igitur* (Therefore, Lord, we pray) for Eucharistic Prayer I; a remembrance of the elect to be inserted in Eucharistic Prayer II; and a prayer for the faithful, that they might lead the elect by word and example, for Eucharistic Prayer III. These are for use in the Masses for all three of the Sundays in which Scrutinies would occur.

If a Scrutiny with children alone is celebrated outside Mass, prayers for the Scrutiny Masses or those given in the rite for children may be used.[10]

Music

For the Scrutinies celebrated with adults, the rite suggests that a song may be sung at the conclusion of the prayer of exorcism; Psalms 6, 26, 32, 38, 39, 40, 51, 116:1–9, 130, 139, and 142 are given as examples, but other songs may be selected, particularly those that highlight forgiveness and mercy. A song at this point helps the elect and the assembly conclude the ritual focused on grace rather than sin.

Many parishes adapt the Intercessions for the Elect to be more specific to the community and the elect. Chanting these may set them apart from the usual intercessions and lend a greater solemnity to them. The individual responsible for the intercessions should collaborate with the musician to adapt them to be sung.

At Mass, if the Universal Prayer and the Creed are to be omitted, the musicians should be made aware that music for the Preparation of the Altar and the Gifts will begin sooner than usual.

---

9. RCIA, 146.
10. RCIA, 296, 300.

Liturgical Environment

The Lenten environment is appropriate for the Scrutinies. Those who tend to the environment should be told what is needed regarding space for the elect to kneel and for the movement of the celebrant among them.

Celebrating the Scrutinies

Introductory Rites

The children and their parents, the adult catechumens (if any), and the godparents may be included in the procession. If it seems appropriate, a shorter form of the Penitential Act could be used. The Collect from either the adult or children's Scrutiny is prayed.

Homily

Guided by the readings and the liturgical texts, the homilist explains the meaning of the Scrutiny in the life of the elect and the parish's spiritual journey. After the homily the elect are called forward with their godparents.

Invitation to Silent Prayer

Addressing the assembly, the celebrant invites them to pray silently "that the elect will be given a spirit of repentance, a sense of sin, and the true freedom of the children of God," as noted in paragraph 152. The elect are invited to bow their heads or kneel. The godparents remain standing. All pray silently "for some time."[11]

Intercessions for the Elect

The adult rite provides two sets of intercessions for each Scrutiny, one very particular to the elect and one that is a bit wider in scope but includes the elect and references the Gospel. The intercessions are mostly stated in the third person plural ("That they"), while those provided in the rite for children are stated in the first person plural ("That we"); it is unclear if the

> The scrutinies are meant to uncover, and then heal all that is weak, defective, or sinful in the hearts of the elect; to bring out, then strengthen all that is upright, strong, and good.
>
> —*Rite of Christian Initiation of Adults*, 141

---

11. RCIA, 152.

prayers are meant to be in the voice of the children or in the voice of the whole assembly.

Many parishes adapt these intercessions to reflect issues of sin and grace raised by the elect as they prepared for these Scrutinies with their parents, godparents, and catechists with the Scriptures to be used at the Scrutiny. The rite allows for these prayers to be combined with the Universal Prayer of the parish community, including intentions for the Church, the world, the poor and the oppressed, and the local community.

These intercessions could be chanted to lend greater solemnity. During the intercessions, the elect remain kneeling (if they have been kneeling) and the parents and godparents place their right hands on the shoulders of the elect.

Exorcism

The Exorcism in the adult Scrutinies consists of two prayers, one addressed to God the Father, the other addressed to Jesus Christ. With the elect still kneeling (if they have been kneeling), the priest celebrant, with folded hands,

After praying the Prayer of Exorcism, the celebrant lays hands on the child.

prays the first prayer while facing the elect. He then lays hands on the elect individually, if this can be done conveniently. This should be done in silence. It is during this part of the rite that the whole Church prays silently but intensely that God will purify, protect, and strengthen these elect. (This should be explained to the community so that they more actively participate in this part of the rite.)

In the children's Scrutiny, there are two options for exorcisms. The first is a single prayer, prayed with hands outstretched over the children. The second is prayed as a dialogue between the priest and the children. This option would require that the children memorize their part or have a printed copy in their hands.

In the Scrutiny for children, an anointing with the Oil of Catechumens may follow the prayer of exorcism, or a laying on of hands may take place.

The rite notes that the anointing may be skipped for pastoral reasons—for example, if the children have already been anointed. Part I of the RCIA does not include the anointing and presumes that the anointing with the Oil of Catechumens will take place possibly several times during the Period of the Catechumenate, ordinarily at a Celebration of the Word of God.[12] Especially if the Scrutiny is celebrated with both adults and children, it would be better to skip the anointing and proceed to the laying on of hands.

Although the rite does not mention it, some parishes ask the parents, companions, godparents, or catechists also to lay hands.

Again, if the Scrutiny is celebrated with both adults and children, it would be better to choose one of the exorcisms from the adult rite, since the children's rite does not include a prayer following the laying on of hands. Instead, the rite proceeds abruptly to the dismissal.

> Along with the children, their godparents and their baptized companions from the catechetical group participate in the celebration of these penitential rites.
>
> —Rite of Christian Initiation of Adults, 293

With hands outstretched, the celebrant then prays the second prayer. The exorcism may conclude with a song of praise for the forgiveness and mercy of God sung by all; the elect stand for this song.

Dismissal of the Elect

The elect and any other catechumens are dismissed in the usual way for further reflection upon the rite and to further contemplate the Word of God that they have heard.

The liturgy continues with the resumption of intercessory prayer unless the Universal Prayer was combined with the Intercessions for the Elect. The Creed may follow the dismissal of the elect or it may be omitted. This deviates from the usual pattern for the Liturgy of the Word in which the Creed follows the homily and the dismissal precedes the Universal Prayer. The ushers, music ministers, and other ministers need to be aware of these changes, since they will affect the timing of the collection and the hymn during the Preparation of the Gifts.[13]

---

12. RCIA, 98, 100.
13. RCIA, 156.

The Presentations

While the Scrutinies are the most notable features of the Period of Purification and Enlightenment, the two ritual Presentations—the Creed and the Lord's Prayer—are important aspects of the enlightenment of the elect during this time. The Presentations sum up and ritualize the entire action of what has taken place during the formation of the elect: their coming to know and accept the Church's teachings and their deepening faith in the one God through a relationship with Jesus Christ. These rites also prepare the elect to take their place among the faithful at worship, particularly in the celebration of the Eucharist, when in the Creed they will profess the faith of the Church and call upon God as Father, as Jesus taught his followers to do. These two actions are the privilege of the baptized.

With the catechumenal formation of the elect completed, the Church lovingly entrusts to them the Creed and the Lord's Prayer, the ancient texts that have always been regarded as expressing the heart of the Church's faith and prayer.

—*Rite of Christian Initiation of Adults*, 147

The chapter "Christian Initiation of Children Who Have Reached Catechetical Age" in the RCIA does not include Presentations adapted for children, although it suggests that the conferences of bishops may do so. Even so, these Presentations are important moments in the children's gradual incorporation into the Church. The Presentations as they appear in Part I are easily adapted for children, and may be celebrated with adults and children at the same time.

Although these presentations are normally celebrated with the elect, they may be celebrated during the catechumenate when the catechumens are judged to be ready. This anticipation is allowed for pastoral reasons: as a "rite of passage" during an extended period of the catechumenate,[14] or for reasons of time, given the shortness of the period of the Period of Purification and Enlightenment.[15]

Preparation for the Presentation of the Creed

As it is described in the *Rite of Christian Initiation of Adults*, the Presentation of the Creed is quite simple. It takes place, preferably, at a weekday Mass with

---

14. 33 §6.
15. RCIA, 104.

special assigned readings, although it may take place at a Celebration of the Word using these same readings. The rite may take place in the church, a smaller chapel, or another place in the parish that can be arranged appropriately. A smaller setting may call for a less formal, but still reverent, celebration.

The defining features of this celebration are the homily on "the meaning and importance of the Creed in relation to the teaching that the elect have already received and to the profession of faith that they must make at their baptism and uphold throughout their lives,"[16] and the profession of the Creed by the assembly in the presence of the elect.

> The Creed, as it recalls the wonderful deeds of God for the salvation of the human race, suffuses the vision of the elect with the sure light of faith.
>
> —*Rite of Christian Initiation of Adults*, 147

The homilist should be aware of the expectation the rite places on the homily and of the assigned readings long before the day of this liturgy. He should also be aware of those for whom this rite is celebrated, whether children alone or children and adults. This is an important moment of catechesis explaining one of the central expressions of our Christian faith. As at the Rite of Sending, if this Presentation is celebrated outside Mass and the celebrant "finds it difficult in the homily to adapt himself to the mentality of children, one of the adults, for example, the children's catechist, may speak to the children after the gospel."[17]

The children should be prepared for this rite by reflecting with their parents, sponsors, godparents, companions, and catechists on the important elements of the faith that are expressed in the Creed. Unfamiliar words might be pointed out and explained. A brief explanation of the rite itself and what will be asked of them is also helpful.

The assembly should be assisted in professing the Creed in a thoughtful and well-paced manner. A worship aid with the Creed printed in sense lines with pauses indicated might be prepared. The celebrant should set a deliberate pace when leading the Creed. The point of this recitation is that the elect hear and understand what is being professed.

When the assembly is professing the Creed, the elect should be standing facing them. Consider where the elect will stand and how they will know

---

16. RCIA, 159.
17. RCIA, 281.

where they are to go. The director of initiation, a catechist, or another person familiar with the rite might guide them at the appropriate moment.

Which Creed is used in this rite? Both the Apostles' Creed and the Nicene Creed are given as options.[18] The Apostles' Creed is essentially the sacramental formula for Baptism, and the more ancient of the two; the Nicene Creed (also called the Niceno-Constantinopolitan Creed) is more theological. The Apostles' Creed is shorter and simpler, and it may make more sense to use it with the children. The Creed that is used should be the one professed on the Sundays of Easter Time so that the newly initiated will be able to participate immediately. Liturgy preparers and celebrants should be asked to use the chosen Creed during this time. Whichever Creed is used in the presentation is to be memorized by the elect and recited as part of the Preparation Rites on Holy Saturday.[19]

The Presentation of the Creed does not call for the giving of a written copy of the Creed as part of the rite. Nothing should interfere with the understanding that the actual presentation is the recitation by the faithful. It is important, however, that the elect have copies of the Creed from which to memorize; it may be appropriate to give them a beautifully printed copy in a session after the presentation is celebrated. If the community uses both Creeds at different times of the year, catechists should explain that and provide a copy of the second Creed as well. Copies of the Creeds should reflect the translations found in the current Missal.

Date and Time

The Presentation of the Creed takes place during the third week of Lent, after the first Scrutiny has been celebrated, preferably at Mass.[20] A regularly scheduled daily Mass, or an additional Lenten Mass, might be the perfect time for this celebration. If circumstances do not permit this, the Presentation could take place at a Liturgy of the Word. In either case, the presence of the community of the faithful is especially significant in this rite. The whole community should know that this event is taking place and that they are welcome and encouraged to be part of it. Because the rite includes a catechetical homily on the Creed, this liturgy might be part of a Lenten event for the whole parish based on the Creed or on particular aspects of it.

---

18. RCIA, 160A, B.
19. RCIA, 193ff.
20. RCIA, 148, 157

Ministers of the Liturgy

Because the rite presumes that the Presentation of the Creed takes place at Mass, the celebrant is a priest. Ideally, the priest is someone who has taken part in the formation of the children and can speak of their growth in the faith that the community will profess in their presence. A deacon may also assist in the liturgy as usual. As at other parish liturgies, readers, servers, a cantor, and other musicians are appropriate ministers.

The celebrant leads the community of the faithful in professing the Creed. This symbolizes that the handing on of the faith to these children has been and continues to be the work of the whole Church. Sponsors, companions, parents, godparents, family members, catechists, and other members of the faithful who have supported the children throughout their journey to faith participate in this rite primarily as members of the assembly.

Music for the Rite

In contrast to some of the other rites of the catechumenal process, the Presentations are fairly simple, amplifying usual parts of the liturgy rather than adding new ones. This celebration should feel like it is part of the parish's celebration of Lent, rather than something apart from it. The Introductory Rites should be similar to those of the Lenten Sundays, although simpler, recognizing that it is a weekday liturgy. If there is a consistent Entrance Chant used on the Sundays of Lent, it might also be appropriate in this case; alternatively, a hymn emphasizing faith would be appropriate. The prescribed Responsorial Psalm for this rite is Psalm 19:8, 9, 10, and 11, with the antiphon "Lord, you have the words of everlasting life." This same psalm is also prescribed for the Easter Vigil, after the sixth Old Testament reading, which provides a lovely connection between the two rites. The verse before the Gospel is John 3:16: "God so loved the world that he gave us his only Son, so that all who believe in him might have eternal life."

Unless the assembly is used to singing the Creed, the Presentation is best done as a recitation. There are some musical settings of this moment that might be considered, but it is important to keep in mind that this proclamation of the Creed belongs to the whole assembly, not to a solo voice to which the assembly responds.

If this rite is celebrated at Mass, the elect are dismissed in the usual way, with the customary music for the dismissal on Sundays. Mass then continues in the usual way.

Celebrating the Presentation of the Creed

The Introductory Rites

The celebrant and other ministers enter as usual. The elect and their parents, sponsors, and/or godparents could be included in the procession or seated in the assembly. The Penitential Act as celebrated throughout Lent is prayed, followed by the Collect. There are no propers designated for the Mass at which the Presentation of the Creed is celebrated. Those for the Lenten weekday on which the rite is celebrated are used.

If the rite is to take place in a smaller setting with fewer people, the Introductory Rites could be simpler, with no procession and a simple Penitential Act. If possible, music should still be incorporated into the celebration.

The Liturgy of the Word

The readings are proclaimed in the usual manner, with the Responsorial Psalm and Gospel Acclamation sung as usual. In place of the readings assigned for the weekday Mass, the readings proclaimed are in the *Lectionary for Mass* under Ritual Masses, I. For the Conferral of Christian Initiation, 1. Catechumenate and Christian Initiation of Adults: 748, Presentation of Creed (Deuteronomy 6:1–7, First Reading; Psalm 19:8, 9, 10, 11, Responsorial Psalm; Romans 10:8–13 or 1 Corinthians 15:1–4 or 1–8a, Second Reading; and Matthew 16:13–18 or John 12:44–50, Gospel). Unlike most weekday Masses, this Mass has a First and Second Reading. The readings should be proclaimed by parish readers or other baptized parishioners who are able to do so.

> My dear friends, listen carefully to the words of that faith by which you will be justified. The words are few, but the mysteries they contain are great. Receive them with a sincere heart and be faithful to them.
>
> —*Rite of Christian Initiation of Adults*, 160

The homily is a pivotal element of this rite. It recounts the growth in faith of the catechumens, now elect, and looks forward to their approaching

Baptism, at which they will profess this faith as the grounding aspect of their lives. It should also address the faithful who are present, preparing them to renew their commitment of faith at Easter.

The Presentation of the Creed

After the homily, the children are called forward by the deacon or another minister. Their parents, sponsors, or godparents need not accompany them, but that is a decision for the catechist and other adults to determine. They face the assembly and are instructed by the celebrant to listen. The celebrant

The Creed is presented to the elect as the assembly prays it.

then recites the first line of the Creed at a moderate pace; the entire assembly joins him in the rest of the Creed. The assembly should be instructed beforehand to maintain the moderate pace and to try to stay together so the children can understand what is said.

Prayer over the Elect

While the children are still in place, the celebrant invites the assembly to pray, and after a few moments of silent prayer, stretches out his hand over them and prays the assigned prayer,[21] which may be modified so the children can understand it better. For example, the invitation to prayer might be rewritten with shorter sentences and easier concepts: Let us pray for these children, that they may know God's love and love him in return. On the day of their Baptism, may God forgive their sins and give them new life in Jesus Christ.

Dismissal

If the Liturgy of the Eucharist is to follow, the elect are dismissed with their catechist or, if they are to stay, they are instructed to stay as a sign of hope. If the Eucharist is not celebrated, all are dismissed. A song may conclude the celebration.

---

21. RCIA, 161.

Preparing the Presentation of the Lord's Prayer

Like the Presentation of the Creed, the Presentation of the Lord's Prayer is quite simple. It takes place, preferably, at weekday Mass with special assigned readings. The rite may take place in the church, a smaller chapel, or another place in the parish that can be arranged appropriately. A smaller setting may call for a less formal, but still reverent, celebration. The proclamation from the Gospel of Matthew in which Jesus teaches his disciples to pray is the actual presentation. When the assembly stands for the proclamation of the Gospel, the elect should also be standing, in front of the assembly, facing the one who is proclaiming the Gospel. Consider where the elect will stand and how they will know where they are to go. The director of initiation, a catechist, or another person familiar with the rite might guide them at the appropriate moment.

The proclamation is followed by a homily that "explains the meaning and importance of the Lord's Prayer."[22] The homilist should be aware of the expectation the rite places on the homily and of the assigned readings long before the day of this liturgy.

The children should be prepared for this rite by reflecting with their parents, sponsors, godparents, companions, and catechists on the meaning of the Lord's Prayer and on what it teaches us about prayer and our relationship to God. Unfamiliar words might be pointed out and explained. A brief explanation of the rite itself is also helpful.

The Presentation of the Lord's Prayer does not call for the giving of a written copy of the prayer as part of the rite. Nothing should interfere with the understanding that the actual presentation is the proclamation of the words of the Lord. It may be appropriate to give the children a beautifully printed copy of the prayer in a session after the presentation is celebrated.

Date and Time

The Presentation of the Lord's Prayer takes place during the fifth week of Lent, after the Third Scrutiny has been celebrated, preferably at Mass.[23] A regularly scheduled daily Mass, or an additional Lenten Mass, might be the perfect time. If circumstances do not permit this, the presentation could take place at a Liturgy of the Word. If the leaders of the Christian initiation process feel it is appropriate, the whole community might be invited to participate.

---

22. RCIA, 181.
23. RCIA, 157.

Because the rite includes a catechetical homily on the Lord's Prayer, this liturgy might be part of a Lenten event for the whole parish based on the Lord's Prayer or on particular aspects of it.

Ministers of the Liturgy

Because the rite presumes that the Presentation of the Lord's Prayer takes place at Mass, the celebrant is a priest. Ideally, the priest is someone who has taken part in the formation of the children and can speak of their growth in their relationship with God and in prayer. A deacon may also assist in the liturgy as usual. As at other parish liturgies, readers, servers, a cantor, and other musicians are appropriate ministers.

Sponsors, godparents, companions, family members, catechists, and other members of the faithful who have supported the elect throughout their journey to faith participate in this rite primarily as members of the assembly.

Music for the Rite

Like the Presentation of the Creed, this celebration should feel like it is part of the parish's celebration of Lent rather than something apart from it. The Introductory Rites should be similar to that of the Lenten Sundays, although simpler, recognizing that it is a weekday liturgy. If there is a consistent Entrance Chant used on the Sundays of Lent, it might also be appropriate in this case; alternatively, a hymn emphasizing our need for God's help or another theme found in the Lord's Prayer. The two options for the Responsorial Psalm for this rite are Psalm 23:1b–3a, 3b–4, 5, 6 with the antiphon "The Lord is my shepherd; there is nothing I shall want" and Psalm 103:1–2, 8 and 10, 11–12, 13 and 14 with the antiphon "As a father is kind to his children, so kind is the Lord to those who fear him." The verse before the Gospel is Romans 8:15: "You have received the Spirit which makes us God's children, and in that Spirit we call God our Father."

If this rite is celebrated at Mass, the elect are dismissed in the usual way, with the customary music for the dismissal on Sundays. Mass then continues in the usual way.

Celebrating the Presentation of the Lord's Prayer

The Introductory Rites

The celebrant and other ministers enter as usual. The elect and their sponsors and/or godparents could be included in the procession or simply seated in the assembly. The Penitential Act as celebrated throughout Lent is prayed, followed by the Collect. There are no designated prayers for the Mass at which the Presentation of the Lord's Prayer is celebrated. Those for the Lenten weekday on which the rite is celebrated are used.

The Liturgy of the Word

The First and Second Readings are proclaimed in the usual manner, with the Responsorial Psalm sung as usual. In place of the readings assigned for the weekday Mass, the readings used are in the *Lectionary for Mass* under Ritual Masses, I. For the Conferral of Christian Initiation, 1. Catechumenate and Christian Initiation of Adults: 749, Presentation of the Lord's Prayer (Hosea 11:1b, 3–4, 8c–9, First Reading; Psalm 23:1–3a, 3b–4, 5, 6 or Psalm 103:1–2, 8 and 10, 11–12, 13 and 18, Responsorial Psalm; Romans 8:14–17, 26–27 or Galatians 4:4–7, Second Reading; and Matthew 6:9–13, Gospel). Unlike most weekday Masses, this Mass has a First and Second Reading.

Following the Second Reading, the elect are called forward by the deacon or another minister and stand facing the ambo. Their sponsors or godparents do not accompany them. The Gospel Acclamation is then sung. Before the proclamation of the Gospel, the celebrant instructs the elect to listen as the Lord teaches his followers how to pray, and the Gospel is proclaimed.

Note that at this place in the Lectionary, the Lord's Prayer in the Gospel reading (Matthew 6:9–13) is the form most commonly prayed by Catholics.

The homily is catechetical in nature, opening up the meaning and importance of the prayer for both the elect and the faithful. As at the Rite of Sending, if this Presentation is celebrated outside Mass and the celebrant "finds it difficult in the homily to adapt himself to the mentality of children, one of the adults, for example, the children's catechist, may speak to the children after the gospel."[24]

---

24. RCIA, 281.

On Holy Saturday, catechists could help the elect in spending time with spiritual materials.

Prayer over the Elect

After the homily, while the elect are still in place, the celebrant invites the assembly to pray, and after a few moments of silent prayer, stretches out his hand over the elect and prays the assigned prayer.

Dismissal

If the Liturgy of the Eucharist is to follow, the elect are dismissed with their catechist or, if they are to stay, they are instructed to do so as a sign of hope. If the Eucharist is not celebrated, all are dismissed. A song may conclude the celebration.

Celebrating the Preparation Rites on Holy Saturday

Finally, the day of the great event, the Easter Vigil, arrives. It is a day of excitement and anticipation for the children and their families and friends. It is also a long day. It would not be unusual for the elect to be caught up in last-minute details with their families, such as housecleaning, shopping, or preparing Easter baskets and special foods for Easter dinner; they may also have the usual commitments that children have on weekends, such as sports, scouting events, school projects, or time with friends. It would be easy for the day to pass into evening with the children tired out and focused on many things.

The *Rite of Christian Initiation of Adults* proposes an alternative vision for the hours preceding the Easter Vigil to help the elect prepare for their initiation: "The elect are to be advised that on Holy Saturday they should refrain from their usual activities, spend their time in prayer and reflection, and, as far as they can, observe a fast."[25] Catechists could assist the elect in deciding how to spend the day by offering spiritual materials to read or watch, reviewing with parents and children the meaning of fasting, and helping them decide how the children and their families might fast together, if appropriate. The catechists might also help the children and their families find quiet times and places on a day when the church itself is likely to be full of activity for at least part of the day.

The best way to help them spend at least part of the day in preparation would be for the elect to gather with parents, godparents, sponsors, companions, catechists, pastors, and other parishioners who have supported them, including other family members and friends, for a time of prayer and preparation. The time together could include a simple walk-through of what the elect will want to know for the evening, such as where they and their families should be seated in the church, where they will change clothes, and where they can leave their dry clothes before the liturgy begins and their wet clothes before it ends. A brief explanation of the movements of the night's liturgy will be helpful, but a detailed rehearsal should not be necessary. Be sure to instruct the children how to receive the Body and Blood of Christ reverently. Assure the children, parents, and godparents that they will be accompanied whenever they need to move. The time together could also include a simple fasting meal, such as soup and bread, and a directive that everyone should take a nap when they get home.

The most important part of the gathering, of course, is prayer. The RCIA offers suggestions for a Celebration of the Word at which one or more preparatory rites may be included:

Celebration of the Word

- the Presentation of the Lord's Prayer, if it has been deferred,
- the "return" or recitation of the Creed,
- the ephphetha rite,
- the choosing of a baptismal name (optional).[26]

This celebration may take place in the church, a chapel, or another space in the parish that can be suitably arranged. General guidelines for Celebrations of the Word are given on pages 43–46 of this book.

---

25. RCIA, 185 §1.
26. RCIA, 185 §2.

Readings and Homily

Each of the preparation rites has suggested readings; one or more of these readings may be chosen for proclamation at this celebration.[27] A suitable psalm or hymn may be sung between the readings if there will be more than one. A brief homily follows.

Presentation of the Lord's Prayer

The Presentation of the Lord's Prayer, which is prescribed to be celebrated during the fifth week of Lent and may be celebrated during the Period of the Catechumenate, is also an option for the Preparation Rites if it has not yet been celebrated. The fact that the RCIA offers three opportunities for the Lord's Prayer to be presented speaks to the importance of this rite. The Lord's Prayer is the essential prayer of Christians, the foundation of all Christian prayer, and the key to understanding who we are as God's children through Baptism into Christ. The newly baptized will pray this prayer publicly with the community for the first time before they receive the Body and Blood of Christ at the Easter Vigil, at every Eucharist and celebration of the Liturgy of the Hours thereafter, and in private prayer. The opportunity to catechize about and celebrate this important prayer should not be omitted from the children's formation.

During the Preparation Rites on Holy Saturday, the elect return the Creed, demonstrating that they know it by heart.

Recitation of the Creed

The Recitation of the Creed may be celebrated if the Presentation of the Creed was celebrated earlier. This rite is also called the "return of the Creed" and demonstrates that the elect know the Creed by heart, symbolizing their reception of the Church's teachings and preparing them to profess their faith at the font through the questions of the baptismal rite and at the Eucharist when the Creed is professed

---

27. Readings for the Recitation of the Creed are listed at RCIA, 194; for the Presentation of the Lord's Prayer, after RCIA, 179; the Ephphetha Rite, at RCIA, 198; and the Choosing of a Baptismal Name, at RCIA, 201.

by the assembly. If this rite and the Ephpheta Rite are both celebrated, the Ephphetha Rite takes place prior to the Prayer before the Recitation.[28]

Ephphetha Rite

The Ephpheta Rite is based on the healing story in Mark 7 in which Jesus opens the ears of a deaf man and cures his speech impediment. "By the power of its symbolism the ephphetha rite, or rite of opening the ears and mouth, impresses on the elect their need of grace in order that they may hear the word of God and profess it for their salvation."[29]

Choosing a Baptismal Name

The Rite of Choosing a Baptismal Name is normally not celebrated in the United States; the United States Conference of Catholic Bishops has decided that it is the norm in the United States that the giving of a new name is not done. The exception is that it may be done at the discretion of the diocesan bishop if the person to be baptized is from a culture in which it is the custom of non-Christian religions to do so.[30] The name chosen may be "either a traditional Christian name or a name of regional usage that is not incompatible with Christian beliefs."[31]

This rite is not a continuation of the practice of taking a Confirmation name, which, although it has not been part of *The Order of Confirmation* for decades, is still practiced in some places. This rite may be adapted, if it seems appropriate, to "consist simply in an explanation of the given name of each of the elect." [32] This might be an opportunity to speak about the Litany of the Saints, which will be sung as part of the baptismal liturgy at the Vigil.

Concluding Rites

A blessing and dismissal conclude the Preparation Rites.[33]

---

28. RCIA, 194.
29. RCIA, 197.
30. RCIA, 33 §4.
31. RCIA, 200.
32. RCIA, 200.
33. RCIA, 203–205.

The Anointing on Holy Saturday

Those who have studied the third edition of *The Roman Missal* may have noticed this rubric in the section "Easter Vigil in the Holy Night," 48:

> After the blessing of baptismal water and the acclamation of the people, the Priest, standing, puts the prescribed questions to the adults and the parents or godparents of the children, as is set out in the respective Rites of the Roman Ritual, in order for them to make the required renunciation. *If the anointing of the adults with the Oil of Catechumens has not taken place beforehand, as part of the immediately preparatory rites, it occurs at this moment* (emphasis added).

This contradicts RCIA, 33.7:

> The National Conference of Catholic Bishops approves the omission of the anointing with the oil of catechumens both in the celebration of baptism and in the optional preparation rites for Holy Saturday. *Thus, anointing with the oil of catechumens is reserved for use in the period of the catechumenate and in the period of purification and enlightenment and is not to be included in the preparation rites on Holy Saturday or in the celebration of initiation at the Easter Vigil or at another time* (emphasis added).

Because the decision of the National Conference of Catholic Bishops (now called the United States Conference of Catholic Bishops) was made in accord with discretionary powers that the *Rite of Christian Initiation of Adults* gives to conferences of bishops, and it was approved by the Holy See, it is particular law for the United States and is not superseded by the third edition of *The Roman Missal*. In short, in the United States, the anointing with the Oil of Catechumens is still reserved to the Period of the Catechumenate and is not done either at the Preparation Rites or at the Easter Vigil.[34]

---

34. Email response to query, Fr. Michael J. Flynn, Secretariat of Divine Worship, United States Conference of Catholic Bishops, February 11, 2016.

Preparing the Celebration of the Sacraments of Initiation

With joy you will draw water from the fountains of salvation.

—Isaiah 12:3

The *Rite of Christian Initiation of Adults* states a preference that the celebration of the sacraments of Christian initiation of children of catechetical age take place at the Easter Vigil.[1] It also recognizes, however, that there may be reasons that this may not be possible. This chapter will first consider how to celebrate Christian initiation at the Vigil, and then how to celebrate it at another time. Whether the sacraments of initiation are celebrated at the Vigil or at another time, the following structure is followed after the homily:

Celebration of Baptism

- Presentation of the Candidates
- Invitation to Prayer
- Litany of the Saints
- Prayer over the Water
- Profession of Faith
  - Renunciation of Sin
  - Profession of Faith
- Baptism
- Explanatory Rites
  - Clothing with a Baptismal Garment (optional)
  - Presentation of a Lighted Candle

---

1. RCIA, 256.

Celebration of Confirmation

- Invitation
- Laying on of Hands
- Anointing with Chrism

The Easter Vigil

The Easter Vigil, in the holy night when the Lord rose again, is considered the "mother of all holy Vigils," in which the Church, keeping watch, awaits the Resurrection of Christ and celebrates it in the Sacraments.[2]

Of all the sacred days and seasons of the liturgical calendar, the Triduum —the Three Days, from the Evening Mass of the Lord's Supper on Holy Thursday through Evening Prayer on Easter Sunday—"shines forth as the high point of the entire liturgical year. Therefore the preeminence that Sunday has in the week, the Solemnity of Easter has in the liturgical year."[3] On the premier liturgy of the preeminent Sunday of the year we celebrate in a particularly festive and solemn way the Paschal Mystery of our Lord Jesus Christ. How fitting it is that we also celebrate the sacraments of initiation by which those who have been journeying with the Church are united to his Death and Resurrection are filled with the Holy Spirit, and are participants in the sacrificial banquet celebrated for the life of the world, and are sent out to bring Good News to the world.

The sanctifying power of this night
dispels wickedness, washes faults away,
restores innocence to the fallen, and joy
to mourners,
drives out hatred, fosters concord, and
brings down the mighty.

—Exsultet, *The Roman Missal*, Easter Vigil, 19

Preparation for the Celebration of the Sacraments of Initiation

The order for the celebration of the sacraments of initiation for children of catechetical age is found at RCIA, 309–329. It is a general outline, adaptable for use at the Vigil or at another celebration; in some places its rubrics differ

---

2. UNLY, 21.
3. UNLY, 18.

from the outline in Part I for the initiation of adults. Since adults usually will be initiated at the Vigil with the children, the recommendations in the following paragraphs will follow Part I.

Liturgical Environment

Those who will be decorating the church for the Vigil should know where the movements of the liturgy will take place. For the rites of initiation, they should know how the elect, in procession or not, will approach the font and the place where Confirmation will occur so that the area is clear. Tables for baptismal garments, candles, and towels for those being baptized, if they are needed, should be strategically placed to be accessible but not prominent; they might be covered with white cloths for uniformity. Holders for the baptismal candles could be arranged so that they might remain burning throughout the Liturgy of the Eucharist, if this is desirable.

Areas with towels for the newly baptized to change into their dry clothes should be available. Plastic bags for wet clothes might be provided. A safe area to store dry clothes before Baptism and wet clothes afterward should be prepared.

Ministers

Minister of Confirmation: The priest or bishop who confers the Sacrament of Baptism on adults and children of catechetical age is also to be the minister of Confirmation when they are celebrated at the same rite. Any time a priest baptizes a person of catechetical age, he is to confirm that person immediately. He does not need special delegation from the bishop; the law itself gives him the faculty.[4] If a large number are to be confirmed, the minister of Confirmation may associate other priests with himself to administer the sacrament.[5]

Assisting Ministers: Initiation ministers or others could be assigned to the elect to accompany them to the various places in the liturgy that they will need to go. They could also assist with chrism, towels, baptismal garments, and candles during the baptismal rite.

For safety reasons, assistants should be prepared with towels to dry off any areas of the floor that are wet from the Baptisms.

---

4. CIC, cc. 883 2°, 885 §2.
5. RCIA, 14, 232.

For a fuller understanding of the effects of Baptism, a font may be constructed that would allow the elect to stand or kneel as water is poured over them.

Ushers should know about and be prepared to help with the various movements of the newly baptized and the whole assembly.

Elect

If the elect are to be baptized by immersion or the pouring of significant amounts of water, as is preferable, they may arrive at the Vigil dressed in simple clothing from which they can easily change. Many parishes provide robes, usually of a dark color, for the elect to wear before and during Baptism.

The Font

> In the celebration of Baptism, the washing with water should take on its full importance as a sign of that mystical sharing in Christ's death and resurrection through which those who believe in his name die to sin and rise to eternal life. Either immersion or the pouring of water should be chosen for the rite . . . to ensure the clear understanding that this washing is not a mere purification rite but the sacrament of being joined to Christ.[6]

If the parish baptismal font does not accommodate Baptism by immersion or allow an adult to stand or kneel while water is poured, a temporary pool could be placed next to the font to allow water from the font to be poured over the heads of those being baptized.

---

6. RCIA, 213.

Research would need to be done into what might serve as an appropriate pool. Whatever is used should be substantial and modestly decorated, an image of the womb of the Church from which emerges a new creation. It should not resemble a wading pool, hot tub, or a shopping-mall fountain. Although impermanent, it is an important element in a sacred action.

Note that the *Rite of Christian Initiation of Adults* directs that the celebration of Baptism should take place within view of the assembly.[7]

Ritual Books

All of the Paschal Vigil is found in *The Roman Missal*, except for the rites of Baptism and Confirmation, which are found in the *Rite of Christian Initiation of Adults*. Be sure that both books are available and marked with ribbons in the appropriate places, and that the servers know which book is needed when.

Celebrating the Sacraments of Initiation at the Easter Vigil

Service of Light

The Church, including the elect, gathers at the fire. Position the elect near the fire, wearing their prebaptismal robes, if these are used, so they can fully experience this powerful symbol and so that they can be symbols of new life to the rest of the assembly. Allow the elect to follow immediately behind the Paschal candle as it leads the assembly into the dark church. Such procession makes sense symbolically because the elect will be the ones who will be made anew on this night by passing through the waters. It also makes sense logistically: if the elect are immediately behind the Paschal candle, they can more easily take their reserved seats as the faithful follow in behind them.

Liturgy of the Word

For the Paschal Vigil, the Lectionary presents nine readings, seven from the Old Testament and two from the New Testament. For pastoral reasons, fewer Old Testament readings may be used; the Exodus reading, however, must always be used.

Proclaiming all the readings may make for a long night for the children, but it is worth considering. These stories tell of God's powerful acts of salvation throughout history. This night the elect are added to this story. No

---

7. RCIA, 218.

matter how many readings are proclaimed, the children should be prepared to hear the readings. The stories could be used in the weeks before the Vigil to help them understand that God has loved the world from the very beginning until this very moment, and that he has wanted them to know and love him all that time.

The readers for the Vigil should be particularly well prepared to proclaim these readings to the children.

Celebration of Baptism

Presentation of the Candidates and the Litany of the Saints

Three options for the presentation of the candidates are provided; the option

In the weeks before the Vigil, the stories in the Holy Saturday readings can be referenced as a way of helping the children understand how God loves us. Familiarity will help the children stay engaged during the many readings.

used depends upon the layout of the parish church and how the Baptisms will take place.[8] No matter which option is chosen, the Litany of Saints is sung by two cantors, with the assembly responding. The Litany may be expanded with additional saints' names, such as the titular saint of the church, patron saints of the elect, or others of particular importance to the community. The music director and the initiation coordinator should be consulted regarding the names of the patron saints of those to be baptized and, perhaps, of those who have accompanied them.

If there will not be a procession to the font, option A is used. The celebrant goes immediately to the font after the homily and the elect are called forward, together with their parents and godparents. With this option, after all have gathered, the celebrant invites the assembly to pray and the Litany of the Saints is sung.

When there is a procession to the font, option B is used. This option calls for the elect to process behind the deacon or other minister carrying the Paschal candle to the font. The celebrant follows the elect and their parents and godparents. During the procession, the Litany of the Saints is sung. This option suits well those churches that have a substantial font with its own space somewhere in the church.

8. RCIA, 219.

In deciding which option to use, consider the liturgical symbolism of a procession. It is a way of praying with our bodies, a physical enactment of our prayer. It symbolizes the great pilgrimage we make to the heavenly Jerusalem, the journey of faith that we make throughout each of our lives, including the journey that the elect have been making in the process of their conversion.

If option B is used, once the procession reaches the font, the celebrant gives the invitation to prayer and the Blessing of Water takes place immediately.

If the parish does not have a substantial font with its own space within the church, or if the font is a fixed font that is located in the sanc-

As the water is being blessed, we hear of the many ways that God has saved us through the use of water.

tuary, option C can be used. With this option, a minister calls the elect forward with their parents and godparents, and the invitation to prayer is given, followed by the Litany of the Saints.

— ● ● —

May this water receive by the Holy Spirit
the grace of your Only Begotten Son,
so that human nature, created in your image
and washed clean through the Sacrament
    of Baptism
from all the squalor of the life of old,
may be found worthy to rise to the life of
    newborn children
through water and the Holy Spirit.

— Blessing of Water, *The Roman Missal*,
Easter Vigil, 46

Both options A and C allow for the Litany of the Saints to be sung after all the elect have been called by name, and while all of them make their way to the font. All three options call for the positioning of the candidates at the font in such a way that the full congregation might witness the Baptisms.

Blessing over Water

Once all have assembled around the baptismal font, the celebrant prays the Prayer over the Water. The Blessing of Water at the Vigil provides a long remembrance of the saving works of God through the element of water, concluding with a prayer for the blessing of the water by the power of the Holy Spirit, followed by an acclamation of the people. This also appears in *The Roman Missal* with a different translation, and either may be used.[9] Decisions about which translation to use rest with the celebrant and the liturgy director. Music for the acclamations should be included in the worship aid for the Vigil; strong leadership by the cantor or choir will help lead the assembly in these acclamations.

Profession of Faith

There are two parts to the Profession of Faith, the renunciation of sin and the profession of faith. "The elect . . . renounce sin and Satan in order to commit themselves for ever to the promise of the Savior and to the mystery of the Trinity."[10] It is important that everyone in the church can hear the elect make this renunciation and profession. In their preparation, the elect might be guided in responding strongly; if needed, microphones could be used.

Either the translation in the *The Roman Missal* or that found in the *Rite of Christian Initiation of Adults* may be used.[11]

The renunciation may be made by the elect as a group or individually.[12] The Profession of Faith is done individually, unless there are "a great many" to be baptized, when the profession may be done in a group. Each of the elect is baptized immediately after making his or her profession.[13]

Baptism

The rite does not specify who should be baptized in what order. The celebrant and initiation leader should determine this. One possible order would be first to baptize any children who have no other family members being bap-

If the method of Baptism is to pour water over the whole body, the elect stands or kneels in the font.

tized during the liturgy. The children who are part of a family group, either siblings or parents or both, would then be baptized with their group. Finally, any adults who are not part of a family group are baptized.

---

9. Letter dated November 30, 2011, by Archbishop Gregory M. Aymond, chairman of the Bishops' Committee on Divine Worship.

10. RCIA, 211.

11. Letter dated November 30, 2011, by Archbishop Gregory M. Aymond, chairman of the Bishops' Committee on Divine Worship.

12. RCIA, 224.

13. RCIA, 225.

An acclamation may be sung after each of the elect is baptized. An "Alleluia," one of the acclamations used during the Blessing of Water, or another acclamation familiar to the assembly may be appropriate; RCIA, 595, offers texts that may be used as acclamations.

Each of the elect comes to the font for Baptism individually. If the method is by immersion, the elect steps into the font. With one or both godparents touching the elect, the priest immerses the elect three times under the water using the customary formulary: "N., I baptize you in the name of the Father," as he immerses the first time; "and of the Son," as he immerses a second time; "and of the Holy Spirit" as he immerses a third time. If the method of Baptism is to pour water over the whole body of the elect (which is a form of immersion), the elect stands or kneels in the font. The priest says, "N., I baptize you in the name of the Father," as he pours water over the head and body a first time; "and of the Son," as he pours water a second time; "and of the Holy Spirit," as he pours a third time.

> In the celebration of baptism the washing with water should take on its full importance as the sign of that mystical sharing in Christ's death and resurrection through which those who believe in his name die to sin and rise to eternal life.
> —*Rite of Christian Initiation of Adults*, 213

Godparents and parents may need to assist the children as they step in and out of the font. Assistants with towels should hand them to the godparents or parents to wrap the children in. If there are several Baptisms taking place, an area away from the font may be prepared with mats where the newly baptized may stand until all have been baptized.

If Baptism is by means of infusion, where the elect approaches the font and leans his or her head over it, then one or both godparents place the right hand on the should of the elect. The celebrant pours water over the forehead three times, saying the formulary as the water is poured. Smaller children may need something to stand on so they can lean their heads over the font.

No matter how the Baptisms are conferred, remember that Christ Jesus stands before us this night, alive in his new members. This is a moment of great joy for the parish community and indeed for the whole Church.

Explanatory Rites

The Explanatory Rites express what God has just done in our midst.[14] Among the Explanatory Rites are the clothing with a baptismal garment and the presentation of a lighted candle. The white baptismal garment "signifies the new dignity" that the neophytes have received and the presentation of the lighted candle shows that the newly baptized are "to walk as befits the children of light."[15]

Clothing with a Baptismal Garment: After all the Baptisms have taken place, an assistant may hand the white robes to the godparents. With the neophytes standing together, their godparents might step forward with white albs or robes folded in their arms. Together the godparents hand the albs to the neophytes while the celebrant says the accompanying prayer, which notes that the neophytes "have been clothed in Christ." The neophytes may be clothed in these garments at this point or, if they have been baptized by immersion, they may wait until they have changed out of their wet clothes.

An assistant should be ready to assist children out of the font and wrap them in a towel.

Presentation of a Lighted Candle: Immediately after the neophytes have received the baptismal garment, the godparents are given a candle. The celebrant calls the godparents forward to light the candle from the Paschal Candle. As with the white garment, the godparents go to the newly baptized and hand them the lighted candles as the celebrant prays the accompanying prayer.

Confirmation

Confirmation is the completion of Baptism, the sealing of that washing with the fullness of the Holy Spirit. Having just been baptized, the neophytes are still standing at the font. Depending on the placement of the font, they may remain there or move to a place in the sanctuary. The priest or bishop who has conferred Baptism is also to confer Confirmation. If many people are to

---

14. RCIA, 227.
15. RCIA, 214.

be confirmed, the priest or bishop may associate other priests to himself to assist in confirming.

The priest or bishop who baptizes a child of catechetical age also confirms that child at the same liturgy.

Any children among the baptized companions who have accompanied the child catechumens to this day who are ready to be confirmed may be confirmed at this time as well.[16] A priest who wishes to confirm a child already baptized in the Catholic Church must obtain permission from the bishop to do so.[17]

If a large number of people are being confirmed, the assembly may sing an appropriate antiphon or hymn during the Confirmation. It may be best to wait until one or two people have been confirmed, so that that assembly is able to hear the words of the sacrament.

Invitation

The celebrant speaks to the newly baptized (and other candidates), explaining the meaning of Confirmation. He then invites the rest of the assembly to pray for the Spirit who will "anoint them to be more like Christ, the Son of God."[18]

A silence of sufficient length to allow for such prayer should follow.

Laying on of Hands and Anointing with Chrism

The celebrant then extends his hands over all those to be confirmed and prays the prayer asking the Father to send the fullness of the Spirit upon them. Then, after being brought the chrism, and in the sight of all the people, their Baptism is confirmed as the celebrant anoints each neophyte on the forehead with the chrism, praying the given formulary, "N., be sealed with the Gift of the Holy Spirit." While this is being done, one or both of the godparents place a hand on the candidate's right shoulder. If several people are being confirmed, the assembly may support the ritual by singing an appropriate antiphon or hymn. Once all are confirmed, and if they were baptized by immersion, they go to change into their white garments.

---

16. RCIA, 256, 322.
17. RCIA, 308.
18. RCIA, 233.

Renewal of baptismal Promises

Invitation

The priest then invites the rest of the assembly to renew their baptismal promises and their Baptism through the sprinkling of the baptismal water. Before the renunciation of sin is made, the candles used at the beginning of the Vigil are relighted from the Paschal candle.

Renunciation of Sin and Profession of Faith: The priest uses the same formulary of renunciation and profession that was used for the elect.

Sprinkling with Baptismal Water

After the profession of faith, the celebrant sprinkles the faithful with the newly blessed baptismal water. The rite prescribes the *Vidi Aquam* (I Saw Water Flowing) for the sprinkling of the people after the Renewal of Baptismal Promises; but another song of a baptismal nature may be sung instead.

The sprinkling should be done with deliberate and full gestures, making sure that everyone in the assembly is sprinkled. Forty days of fasting, prayer, and almsgiving has led the baptized to this moment. In many parishes, the entire assembly is invited to the baptismal font to renew their Baptism, in place of the sprinkling, although this is not mentioned in the rite.

With deliberate and full gestures, the celebrant sprinkles the faithful with the newly blessed baptismal water.

Return of the Neophytes to the Assembly

If the neophytes left the assembly to dry off and change clothes, they should return to the assembly before the Universal Prayer (the Prayer of the Faithful). They should be wearing their white garments and carrying their lighted baptismal candles as they process in. As they return to the assembly, they should be greeted with joyful music, possibly an acclamation or refrain that lasts until they take their places. They may extinguish their candles or put them in a place prepared for them.

The Liturgy of the Eucharist

Finally in the celebration of the Eucharist, as the newly baptized take part for the first time and with full right, they reach the culminating point in their Christian initiation. In this Eucharist the neophytes, now raised to the ranks of the royal priesthood, have an active part both in the general intercessions and, to the extent possible, in bringing the gifts to the altar. With the entire community they share in the offering of the sacrifice and say the Lord's Prayer, giving expression to the spirit of adoption as God's children that they have received in baptism. When in communion they receive the body that was given for us and the blood that was shed, the neophytes are strengthened in the gifts they have already received and are given a foretaste of the eternal banquet.[19]

The newly baptized may bring forth the gifts at the Easter Vigil.

The rite notes a number of things about the celebration of the Eucharist on this night. Even though the Litany of the Saints was prayed, on this night the Universal Prayer is prayed so the newly baptized may take part, exercising their baptismal priesthood for the first time.[20] On this night, it is most appropriate that the newly baptized bring forth the gifts. And on this night they pray the Lord's Prayer with the entire community, "giving expression to the spirit of adoption as God's children that they have received in baptism."[21]

> To signify clearly the interrelation . . . of the three sacraments which are required for full Christian initiation (canon 842:2), adult candidates, including children of catechetical age, are to receive baptism, confirmation, and eucharist in a single eucharistic celebration.
>
> *National Statutes for the Catechumenate*, 14

Any children among the baptized companions who have accompanied the child catechumens to this day who are ready to receive the Eucharist for the first time may do so at this Mass.[22]

---

19. RCIA, 217.
20. RCIA, 241.
21. RCIA, 217.
22. RCIA, 256, 322.

Special interpolations are given in the *The Roman Missal* at Ritual Masses, Christian Initiation: Baptism, for Eucharist Prayers I, II, and III. These interpolations reference the newly baptized and their godparents.[23] Before the Lamb of God, the celebrant may speak briefly to the newly baptized, reminding them of the preeminence of the Eucharist in their lives now that they are initiated. Finally, the Rite notes that it is most fitting for the newly baptized to come forward in the Communion procession first, to receive the Bread of Life and the Cup of Salvation; that is, Communion under both kinds.[24]

It is appropriate for the newly baptized to be among the first in the congregation to receive the Eucharist.

Celebrating Initiation outside the Easter Vigil

When the sacraments of initiation with children are celebrated at a time other than the Easter Vigil, the rite prefers that the celebration take place on a Sunday, "the day that the Church devotes to the remembrance of Christ's resurrection."[25]

The readings may be taken from the *Lectionary for Mass*, 751, "Celebration of the Sacraments of Initiation apart from the Easter Vigil" or from the Sunday or feast on which the celebration takes place.[26] An Old Testament reading from the Easter Vigil may also be chosen.[27] The Mass of the day or the Ritual Mass "For the Conferral of Baptism" is used.[28]

After the homily, the celebration proceeds much as it does at the Easter Vigil, with a few changes.

Chapter 1 of Part II offers one interesting addition: the baptized members of the community may profess their faith by reciting the Creed before the children profess

In accord with the ancient practice followed in the Roman liturgy, adults are not to be baptized without receiving confirmation immediately afterward, unless some serious reason stands in the way.

—*Rite of Christian Initiation of Adults*, 215

23. RCIA, 242.
24. RCIA, 243.
25. RCIA, 304.
26. RCIA, 306.
27. *Lectionary for Mass*, 751.
28. RCIA, 306.

their faith using the usual baptismal formula of renunciation and profession. This is done not only for the renewal of their faith, but also as a reminder that they must be ready to assist the children as they grow in the faith into which they are about to be initiated.

One of both of the godparents places the right hand on the candidate's shoulder during Confirmation.

The celebration of Baptism and Confirmation then proceeds as at the Vigil. Whether or not the community professed their faith before the children, the renewal of baptismal promises and the sprinkling are not done.

If the children have been baptized by immersion, consideration will have to be given to how and when they will change into dry clothes. An appropriate hymn of praise could follow the conferral of Confirmation so that the neophytes can change.

The Universal Prayer is after the conferral of Confirmation. This is the first time the children will take place in this duty of the baptized.

The newly baptized may take part in the Presentation of the Gifts.

Period of Mystagogy

The *Rite of Christian Initiation of Adults* refers to the newly baptized as *neophytes*, a word that comes from the Greek for "new plants." Like new plants, the neophytes need tending as they take their places as full members of the Church.

> This is a time for the community and the neophytes together to grow in deepening their grasp of the paschal mystery and in making it part of their lives through meditation on the Gospel, sharing in the Eucharist, and doing the works of charity. To strengthen the neophytes as they begin to walk in newness of life, the community of the faithful, their godparents, and their parish priests (pastors) should give them thoughtful and friendly help.[29]

This description of the Period of Mystagogy closely matches paragraph 75 of the RCIA, which describes the training in the Christian life that is to take place during the Period of the Catechumenate in four ways: catechesis

---

29. RCIA, 244.

accommodated to the liturgical year and supported by the Word of God; learning the Christian way of life from the community; celebration of liturgical rites; and participating in the apostolic life of the Church. Both paragraphs describe parish life as much as they describe periods of formation. The catechumenate, then, is the time when catechumens learn to believe and live as the Church believes and lives. The Period of Mystagogy is when they, as baptized believers, begin to live the Christian life fully, centered in personal experience of the Eucharist.

For this reason, the Sunday Masses of Easter Time are the main setting for mystagogy. "Besides being occasions for the newly baptized to gather with the community and share in the mysteries, these celebrations include particularly suitable readings from the Lectionary, especially the readings for Year A."[30] Of course, the homilist will need to preach the Scriptures of Easter Time in light of the presence of the neophytes, but even when there are no neophytes, the Sundays of Easter are the premier time for focusing on the centrality of the Eucharist in the Christian life.

Throughout Easter Time, the neophytes are together in a special place during worship.

The intensity of Holy Week itself, with its Paschal Triduum, followed by the joyful celebration of fifty days that climax in Pentecost, is an excellent time for the homilist to draw links between the Scriptures and the Eucharist. It was precisely in the "breaking of the bread"—which recalled Jesus' total gift of self at the Last Supper and then upon the Cross—that the disciples realized that their hearts burned within them as the risen Lord opened their minds to the understanding of the Scriptures. A similar pattern of understanding is to be hoped for still today. The homilist works diligently to explain the Scriptures, but the deeper meaning of what he says will emerge in "the breaking of the bread" at that same liturgy if the homilist has built bridges to that moment.[31]

---

30. RCIA, 247.
31. *Homiletic Directory*, 54.

In addition, the neophytes and their godparents sit together in a special place throughout Easter Time in the assembly, and prayers for them are included in the Universal Prayer.

———————●●—————————

A period of postbaptismal catechesis or mystagogy should be provided to assist the young neophytes and their companions who have completed their Christian initiation.

—*Rite of Christian Initiation of Adults*, 330

The Second Sunday of Easter was at one time known as *Dominica in alba depositis*, signifying that the neophytes, who wore their white garments for a week after Easter while they were catechized about the meaning of the initiation rites they had experienced, set their robes aside on this day, appearing the same as the rest of the assembly. The liturgy still acknowledged their presence. The introit, based on chapter 2 of the First Letter of St. Peter, was *Quasi modo geniti infantes, rationabile, sine dololac concupiscite*.[32] This is still one of the two Entrance Antiphons given for this day in *The Roman Missal*: "Like newborn infants, you must long for the pure, spiritual milk that in him you may grow to salvation, alleluia."

We can glean two things from this. First, the neophytes need to make sense of all that happened to them at the Easter Vigil and in everything that led up to it. Having received the sacraments, they can understand their meanings more deeply than they could before. The homilies of Easter Time can certainly address some of this, but it is important to gather the neophytes a few times to reflect on the sacramental symbols. These sessions can be informal, guided discussions rather than lessons. Prayer incorporating Scripture and the symbols of Easter should be part of such sessions. Videos and photos of the event may help call to mind each person's experience of the events. And food always encourages sharing.

The second thing we can glean is that the neophytes will be "newbies" for quite some time. They will still need support. While the formal time of mystagogy lasts for the fifty days until Pentecost, the bishops of the United States direct that

After the immediate mystagogy or postbaptismal catechesis during the Easter season, the program for the neophytes should extend until the anniversary of Christian initiation, with at least monthly assemblies

---

32. The Sunday came to be known as *Quasimodo* Sunday. In Victor Hugo's novel, *The Hunchback of Notre Dame,* the abandoned infant was said to have been found on this Sunday and given the name Quasimodo.

of the neophytes for their deeper Christian formation and incorporation into the full life of the Christian community.[33]

Like the immediate mystagogical gatherings, these can be informal times of prayer and conversation.

"On the anniversary of their baptism the neophytes should be brought together in order to give thanks to God, to share with one another their spiritual experiences, and to renew their commitment."[34] The anniversary of the neophytes' initiation is the next year's Easter Vigil, even though it isn't exactly the same date. They should certainly be encouraged to be there to rejoice with the newly baptized and to recall their initiation with a deeper understanding.

Many dioceses have a Mass for the neophytes with the bishop during the Easter season. If this is the case, the neophytes and their godparents should be encouraged to go.

We continue to break open the mysteries throughout our lives as we ponder the Gospel, receive the Eucharist, and do works of charity.

Should the bishop come to the parish in the course of the year, try to arrange for him to meet the neophytes. If possible, have them sit together at a Mass at which the bishop presides.

In many ways, all of Christian life is mystagogical. We are always gaining deeper understanding of the Paschal Mystery through meditation on the Gospel, sharing in the Eucharist, and doing works of charity. It is the life of the Church until we come face to face with the Divine Mystery at our death.

33. NS, 24.
34. RCIA, 250.

Preparing the Rites for Uncatechized, Baptized Children

> While I am in the world, I am the light of the world.
>
> —John 9:5

The *Rite of Christian Initiation of Adults* is primarily concerned with the initiation of the unbaptized, but within the text also are rites through which the baptized receive the Sacraments of Confirmation and Eucharist. Chapter 4 of Part II of the RCIA is concerned with preparing adults who were baptized either in the Roman Catholic Church or in another Christian community but were never catechized.[1]

For a Roman Catholic this presumes someone who never received Confirmation and Eucharist. A person who received first Communion is presumed to have received some catechesis in the faith before receiving the sacrament. For a non-Catholic, this is someone who was baptized in early childhood who never attended church services or participated in Sunday school or other religious formation regularly and now seeks to be received into the full communion of the Catholic Church. Chapter 4, "Preparation of Uncatechized Adults for Confirmation and Eucharist," offers a plan of catechesis that "for the most part . . . corresponds to the one laid down for catechumens (see no. 75.1)."[2] But what about an uncatechized, baptized Catholic child?

Preparing Uncatechized Children Baptized in the Catholic Church for Confirmation and Eucharist

It may be appropriate for children who were baptized Catholic, but "did not receive further catechetical formation nor, consequently, the sacraments of confirmation and eucharist"[3] to follow a catechumenate-like process, but discernment is very important. The background and religious history of the

---

1. See RCIA, 400–472.
2. RCIA, 402.
3. RCIA, 400.

child and the family, as well as the age of the child, need to be taken into consideration when deciding if this is the best option. The question revolves around the interpretation of "further catechetical formation."

The Church is saying that if the child has been baptized in the Roman Catholic Church but never or rarely attended Mass and received no formation in faith, that child, after reaching catechetical age, would most likely follow a plan similar to the catechumenate. It is fairly easy to discern when the child has had no catechetical formation.

Discernment is not as easy when the amount of formation is not as clear. Often the baptized Catholic child and the family have attended Mass occasionally and have had some catechetical formation, even if not in a formal religious education class. This is when wise pastoral discernment is necessary, and clear communication is key.

It is helpful to remember that liturgy is formative. If the family has attended Mass, even sporadically, then they have been practicing their faith, albeit irregularly. Even though formation may not have occurred in a formal catechetical setting, the child has received some formation by participating in the liturgy. If one or both of the parents are baptized Catholic and culturally Catholic, they have likely passed along some elements of the faith. Talking with the child and parents about their faith journey, their prayer life, and their relationship with God and the Church will help determine whether a catechumenate-like experience is the best option for this baptized Catholic child.

In some instances, the best option is for the Catholic child to receive appropriate sacramental catechesis that prepares her or him for the Sacraments of Penance and Eucharist, and possibly Confirmation. After adequate sacramental catechesis, and assuming the child is participating in religious education and Sunday worship, the child would receive the Sacraments of Penance, Eucharist, and Confirmation in accord with diocesan guidelines.

> Even though uncatechized adults have not yet heard the message of the mystery of Christ, their status differs from that of catechumens, since by baptism they have already become members of the Church and children of God.
>
> —Rite of Christian Initiation of Adults, 400

If it is discerned that the child would benefit from a catechumenate-like catechesis, it must always be kept in mind that "their status differs from that of catechumens, since by baptism they have already become members of the Church and children of God. Hence their conversion is based on the baptism they have already received, the effects of which they must develop."[4]

Once they have entered into formation for the celebration of the Sacraments of Confirmation and Eucharist, they attend the Sunday Eucharist weekly.[5] If their families are not participating in the Eucharist, the children should attend Mass with an adult sponsor or a child companion and their family. Even though these children are not yet sufficiently formed to receive

the Body and Blood of Christ in Holy Communion, they can participate in the priestly actions of interceding for the world and praying the Eucharistic Prayer. Although some parishes dismiss baptized candidates at the same time as catechumens, a better approach may be to spend time early in the child's formation, separate from the catechumens, to understand how their Baptism has prepared them to participate in the prayer of the Church and how to do so until the time they can receive Holy Communion. The baptized may participate in the catechesis and other activities prepared for the catechumens as appropriate.

For some uncatechized Catholic children, Eucharist and Confirmation are received according to diocesan guidelines after appropriate catechesis is provided.

During the time of preparation some or all of the optional rites found in chapter 4 of Part II may be celebrated with the children, possibly at the same time as they are celebrated with uncatechized adults. Because these rites are optional, the initiation directors should discern with the parents, sponsors, and catechists whether they would be beneficial. These rites are described later in this chapter.

When these children are sufficiently catechized and their faith is of sufficient maturity, they are to be confirmed and receive the Eucharist at the same time. The children, according to their own consciences, "should make

---

4. RCIA, 400.
5. RCIA, 413.

a confession of sins beforehand."[6] The children's reception of Confirmation and Eucharist does not necessarily take place at the Easter Vigil, although it may[7]; some parishes, however, reserve that celebration for those to be baptized. Because the children are already Catholic, they must be confirmed by a bishop unless the priest has obtained explicit permission from the bishop to confirm them.[8] They may also

Children who were baptized in the Roman Catholic Church but were then uncatechized may receive Confirmation and Eucharist when the bishop confirms other children of the parish.

celebrate their Confirmation and Eucharist when the bishop confirms other children of the parish.

Uncatechized Children Who Were Baptized in Other Christian Traditions Seeking Reception into the Full Communion of the Catholic Church

A child to be received into the full communion of the Catholic Church who was baptized in another Christian tradition in early childhood but never or rarely attended church services or participated in Sunday school or other religious formation regularly most likely will need a catechumenate-like catechetical experience. As with an uncatechized Catholic child, however, it would be prudent to discern the child's real needs. He or she may have been introduced to some Scripture and basic Christian teaching and have formed the beginnings of a relationship with God.

For a child with little or no familiarity with the Catholic Church, religious education classes may not, at least at first, be appropriate. It is important, however, that the child get to know other children from the parish. Catholic companions might join with the child preparing for reception, just as they do with child catechumens.

In the case of a child seeking reception into the Catholic Church, often a parent or other family members also are seeking to be received. It may be

6. RCIA, 482.
7. RCIA, 409.
8. RCIA, 409; CIC, c. 884.

best to work with the family as a group, with a Catholic family as sponsors and companions.

Once the children have entered into formation for the reception and celebration of the Sacraments of Confirmation and Eucharist, they attend the Sunday Eucharist weekly.[9] If their families are not participating in the Eucharist, the children should attend Mass with an adult sponsor or a child companion and their family. Though not yet sufficiently formed to receive the Body and Blood of Christ in Holy Communion, the children can participate in the priestly actions of interceding for the world and praying the Eucharistic Prayer. Although some parishes dismiss baptized candidates at the same time as catechumens, a better approach may be to spend time early in the child's formation, separate from the catechumens, to understand how their Baptism has prepared them to participate in the prayer of the Church and how to do so until the time they can receive Holy Communion. The baptized may participate in the catechesis and other activities prepared for the catechumens as appropriate.

> For the most part the plan of catechesis corresponds to the one laid down for catechumens (see no. 75.1). But in the process of catechesis the priest, deacon, or catechist should take into account that these adults have a special status because they are baptized.
>
> —*Rite of Christian Initiation of Adults*, 402

During the time of preparation some or all of the optional rites found in chapter 4 of Part II may be celebrated with the children, possibly at the same time as they are celebrated with uncatechized adults. Because these rites are optional, the initiation directors should discern with the parents, sponsors, and catechists whether they would be beneficial. These rites are described later in this chapter.

When these children are sufficiently catechized and their faith is of sufficient maturity, they are received using the Rite of Reception into the Full Communion of the Catholic Church, which is discussed in the next chapter. The children, according to their own consciences, "should make a confession of sins beforehand."[10] The children's reception and celebration of Confirmation and Eucharist does not necessarily take place at the Easter Vigil, although it

---

9. RCIA, 413.
10. RCIA, 482.

may[11]; some parishes, however, reserve that celebration for those to be baptized. This rite may take place at any time, normally at a celebration of the Eucharist.[12] Most parishes celebrate it at a Sunday Mass. Reception into the Catholic Church is followed immediately by the celebration of Confirmation. The priest who receives an adult or child of catechetical age into the Catholic Church has the faculty to confirm and must use it in this situation.[13]

Baptized, Catechized Children Seeking Reception into the Full Communion of the Catholic Church

Baptized children who have been active members of a Christian community do not take part in a catechumenate-like catechetical process because their situation is not parallel to catechumens. They do not celebrate the optional rites found in chapter 4 of Part II, which are adapted from the rites for catechumens. The children are practicing, faithful, baptized Christians.

Discernment is part of this process, though it is different for that done with catechumens. Here, parents and children, along with the pastor or a catechist, should consider the formation that is needed. The Rite of Reception into the Full Communion of the Catholic Church notes that "no greater burden than necessary is required"[14] to receive an individual into the Catholic Church.

In the case of a child seeking reception into the Catholic Church, there is often a parent or other family members also seeking to be received. It may be best to work with the family as a group, with a Catholic family as sponsors and companions.

Once they have entered into formation for the celebration of the Sacraments of Confirmation and Eucharist, they attend the Sunday Eucharist weekly.[15] If their families are not participating in the Eucharist, the children should attend Mass with an adult sponsor or a child companion and their family. Even though the child is not yet sufficiently formed to receive the Body and Blood of Christ in Holy Communion, they can participate in the priestly actions of interceding for the world and praying the Eucharistic Prayer.

---

11. RCIA, 409.
12. RCIA, 475 §1.
13. CIC, cc. 883 2°, 885 §2.
14. RCIA, 473.
15. RCIA, 413.

When these children are ready, they are received using the Rite of Reception into the Full Communion of the Catholic Church, which is discussed in the next chapter. The children, according to their own consciences, "should make a confession of sins beforehand."[16] The rite of reception may take place at any time, normally at a celebration of the Eucharist.[17] Most parishes celebrate it at a Sunday Mass. Reception into the Catholic Church is followed immediately by the celebration of Confirmation. The priest who receives an adult or child of catechetical age into the Catholic Church has the faculty to confirm and must use it in this situation.[18]

Optional Rites for Baptized but Uncatechized Adults

The Church provides optional liturgical celebrations to mark the preparation for the sacraments of Confirmation and Eucharist and reception into full communion. The first of these rites, the Rite of Welcoming the Candidates, welcomes into the life of the community those seeking to complete their initiation or be received into full communion. It acknowledges that, because of their Baptism, these candidates are already part of the community. The next rite, the Rite of Sending the Candidates for Recognition by the Bishop and Call for Continuing Conversion provides a chance for the community to "express its joy in the candidates' decision," as noted in paragraph 435, and to send them to the cathedral where the bishop will recognize them. A penitential rite will mark the candidates' Lenten journey. This penitential rite is different from than the Scrutiny in which the catechumens participate. The penitential rite may help in preparing these candidates for the Sacrament of Penance.

These optional rites are reserved for the uncatechized. As *National Statutes*, 31, states, "Those baptized persons who have lived as Christians and need only instruction in the Catholic tradition and a degree of probation within the Catholic community should not be asked to undergo a full program parallel to the catechumenate."

---

16. RCIA, 482.
17. RCIA, 475 §1.
18. Canons, 883, 885.

Celebrating the Rite of Welcoming the Candidates

This optional rite usually takes place at a Sunday Eucharist, but may also take place at a Celebration of the Word of God. If this rite is to take place at a Sunday liturgy, a date should be chosen when the Scriptures of the day are appropriate for the purpose of the rite. If this rite is not celebrated, the candidates should be introduced to the community in another appropriate manner.

This rite is similar to the Rite of Acceptance into the Order of Catechumens, but it is simpler.[19] The liturgy begins in the usual way, with a procession of ministers. Because

> The prayers and ritual gestures [of the Rite of Welcoming] acknowledge that such candidates are already part of the community because they have been marked by baptism.
>
> —*Rite of Christian Initiation of Adults*, 412

these children are baptized, they already have a place among the faithful,[20] where they are seated as the liturgy begins. The Mass begins with the Entrance Song and then continues with the rite as following:

Welcoming the Candidates

- Greeting
- Opening dialogue
- Candidate's declaration of intent
- Affirmation by the sponsors and the assembly
- Signing of the candidates with the cross
  - Signing of the forehead
  - Signing of the other senses (optional)
  - Concluding prayer

Liturgy of the Word

- Instruction
- Readings
- Homily
- Presentation of a Bible (optional)
- Profession of Faith

---

19. See the section on preparing the Rite of Acceptance in to the Order of Catechumens, pages 22–41 in this book.
20. RCIA, 416.

- Universal Prayer
- Prayer over the Candidates

Greeting: After the Entrance Procession, the celebrant greets the children and the whole assembly, whom he reminds that the new people among them are baptized. He then invites the candidates and their parent(s) or sponsors to come forward. If there is a large number of candidates, music may accompany this movement. The rite suggests Psalm 63:1–8.

Care should be taken to place the candidates in such a way that they can be seen by all in the assembly; if necessary, microphones should be provided so that all may hear their responses.

Opening Dialogue: The celebrant could ask each candidate his or her name, and each could then give his or her name; or he could call out their names for them to reply "Present." But perhaps it would be more comfortable for the children if the parents, godparents, or sponsors, introduced the children. The celebrant would then inquire from the children what they ask of the Church. The children should be prepared to answer in their own words that they wish to be accepted for preparation leading to Confirmation and Eucharist or to reception into the full communion of the Catholic Church.

Candidates' Declaration of Intent and Affirmation by the Sponsors and the Assembly: The celebrant then asks the candidates to state their desire to continue the journey of faith, either in response to his question or in their own words.[21] He then asks the parents or sponsors and assembly if they are ready to assist the candidates.

Signing of the Candidates with the Cross: The celebrant marks the children with the cross on their foreheads, with words that indicate that this is a reminder of their Baptism. The parents, sponsors, companions, or catechist may also sign them. An acclamation may be sung, as at the Rite of Acceptance.

The celebrant may then sign the other senses as at the Rite of Acceptance. In preparing this liturgy, the initiation ministers and celebrant may wish to discuss whether the multiple signing is appropriate for the children because of either cultural issues or the children's comfort level.[22]

---

21. See RCIA, 419.
22. RCIA, 33 §3. The Canadian version of this rite includes only the signing of the forehead.

Liturgy of the Word

After a brief instruction to the candidates, the Word is proclaimed in the usual way and the homily is preached on the Scriptures, taking into account the presence of those beginning their preparations.

Presentation of a Bible: After the homily, candidates may be called forward so that the celebrant may present them a Bible (or a book containing the Gospels). This may be a Bible that is given for each to keep, or it may be a large Bible or the *Book of the Gospels* used at Mass that is presented in a ritual manner and then reverenced by each candidate in turn. An acclamation could accompany this action. This rite is optional.

Profession of Faith: The Creed is recited on Sundays and solemnities.

Universal Prayer and Prayer over the Candidates: Intercessions for the candidates are included in the Universal Prayer, which concludes with a prayer prayed by the celebrant with hands outstretched over the candidates.

Dismissal of the Assembly or Liturgy of the Eucharist: If the Eucharist is not celebrated, all are dismissed. If the Liturgy of the Eucharist is celebrated, it begins as usual with the Preparation of the Gifts. The candidates are not dismissed, nor do they present the gifts.

Rite of Sending the Candidates for Recognition by the Bishop and the Call to Continuing Conversion

This rite[23] may be celebrated when the children will be sent to the diocesan celebration of the Rite of Calling the Candidates to Continuing Conversion.

It is celebrated prior to the Rite of Calling, usually at a Sunday Eucharist or a Celebration of the Word. It is similar to the optional Rite of Sending Catechumens for Election, but simpler; see notes on that rite on pages 54–57. The rite does not call for the signing of the Book of the Elect by the candidates; parishes should follow the practice of their diocese.

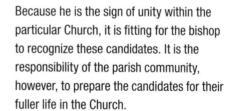

Because he is the sign of unity within the particular Church, it is fitting for the bishop to recognize these candidates. It is the responsibility of the parish community, however, to prepare the candidates for their fuller life in the Church.

—*Rite of Christian Initiation of Adults*, 435

---

23. RCIA, 434–445.

Presentation of the Candidates: After the homily, the minister in charge of the formation of the children presents them to the celebrant for recognition of the progress they have made and the assurance of the community's prayers. The candidates are called forward by name and go forward with their parents or sponsors to the celebrant. They should stand so that the assembly may see their faces.

Affirmation by the Sponsors and the Assembly: The priest asks the parents, sponsors, and assembly to affirm the readiness of the candidates.

Universal Prayer and Prayer over the Candidates: Intentions for the candidates are prayed, which conclude with a prayer by the celebrant, prayed with hands outstretched over the candidates. If this rite takes place at a celebration of the Eucharist, the usual intercessions for the Church and the world may be included.

Dismissal of the Assembly or Liturgy of the Eucharist: If the Eucharist is not celebrated, everyone is dismissed. If the Liturgy of the Eucharist is celebrated, it begins as usual with the Preparation of the Gifts. The candidates are not dismissed, nor do they present the gifts. For pastoral reasons, the profession of faith may be omitted.[24]

Penitential Rite (Scrutiny)

The RCIA offers the option of celebrating the Penitential Rite for the baptized candidates.[25] It is designed to be celebrated on the Second Sunday of Lent, but it may be celebrated on a Lenten weekday or at another suitable time. If the Penitential Rite is celebrated on the Second Sunday of Lent, the Mass and the readings of that day are used; if it is celebrated on another day, appropriate readings from the Lectionary are used[26] and the Collect provided in the rite is prayed.[27] This rite follows a pattern similar to the Scrutinies; instead of focusing on preparation for Baptism, however, the texts and prayers focus on preparation for

———●●●———

This penitential rite is intended solely for celebrations with baptized adults preparing for confirmation and eucharist or reception into the full communion of the Catholic Church.

—*Rite of Christian Initiation of Adults*, 463

---

24. RCIA, 445.
25. RCIA, 459–472.
26. RCIA, 466.
27. RCIA, 465.

Reconciliation. The candidates will receive the Sacrament of Reconciliation before they are confirmed, share in the Eucharist, and (if appropriate) are received into the full communion of the Catholic Church.

Suggestions for celebrating the Scrutinies may help in planning this rite.[28] There is no ritual Mass for the Penitential Rite as there are for the Scrutinies. There is no combined rite for the Scrutinies and the Penitential Rite. The prayers and other texts of the Scrutinies are specific to the elect; they include prebaptismal exorcisms, which are not appropriate to the baptized.

Celebrating the Penitential Rite (Scrutiny)

Introductory Rites: During the Introductory Rites, the celebrant "explains that the rite will have different meanings for the different participants . . . particularly those who are preparing to celebrate the sacrament of penance for the first time. . . . All . . . are going to hear the comforting message of pardon for sin, for which they will praise the Father's mercy."[29]

Invitation to Silent Prayer: After the homily, the children are called forward with their parents or sponsors. After instructions to the assembly and the candidates to pray in silence, the priest invites the candidates to bow their heads or to kneel. The parents or sponsors remain standing; the assembly remains seated. The entire community prays silently for the candidates; after a substantial period of silence, all stand for the intercessions.

Universal Prayer and Prayer over the Candidates: Intentions for the candidates are prayed; if this rite takes place at a celebration of the Eucharist, the usual intercessions for the Church and the world may be included. After the intercessions, the celebrant prays aloud, with hands outstretched over the candidates. Two Prayers over the Candidates are provided; option A is most appropriate on the Second Sunday of Lent.

Dismissal of the Assembly or Liturgy of the Eucharist: If the Eucharist is not celebrated, all are dismissed. If the Liturgy of the Eucharist is celebrated, it begins as usual with the Preparation of the Altar and the Gifts. The candidates are not dismissed, nor do they present the gifts. For pastoral reasons, the profession of faith may be omitted.[30]

---

28. These are found on pages 58–65.
29. RCIA, 464.
30. RCIA, 472.

Preparing the Rite of Reception of Baptized Christians

Then the two recounted what had taken place on the way and
how he was made known to them in the breaking of the bread.

—Luke 24:35

When a person who was baptized in another Christian community
desires to become Catholic, the individual is received into the Church
through the Rite of Reception of Baptized Christians into the Full
Communion of the Catholic Church. This rite[31] originally existed apart from
the *Rite of Christian Initiation of Adults*. When the Church reestablished the
catechumenal process of initiation, the rite was included in the RCIA to
address the needs of the baptized who sought unity with the Catholic Church.

The purpose of this rite is to establish communion and unity with those
who are validly baptized in another Christian community and seek to be
received into the fullness of communion. Children who have been baptized
in another Christian community may or may not need an extended period
of catechesis in preparation for reception, as noted in the previous chapter.
Those who need an extended period of catechesis are prepared according
to the process indicated in Part II, chapter four, "Preparation of Uncatechized Adults for Confirmation and Eucharist" and *National Statutes*, 31, "adapted to the age and circumstances of the child."[32] Each child should have a parent and/or sponsor to accompany him or her in the process of formation. For a number of reasons, it may be helpful for a sponsor to accompany the child. If the family is new to the parish, for instance, a sponsor could help introduce both the parent

> The sacrament of baptism cannot be repeated and therefore it is not permitted to confer it again conditionally, unless there is a reasonable doubt about the fact or validity of the baptism already conferred.
>
> —*Rite of Christian Initiation of Adults*, 480

31. RCIA, 473–504.
32. RCIA, 400–472.

and child to other parishioners. The sponsor for the celebration of Confirmation should be someone other than a parent.

For those baptized persons who are seeking full communion, there is no specified time for reception. While many parishes receive baptized Christians at the Vigil, this is not necessary. In fact, the *National Statutes for the Catechumenate* state that "it is preferable that reception into full communion not take place at the Easter Vigil."[33]

Rather, the reception of baptized Christians may take place at any time during the year, "at the Sunday Eucharist of the parish community."[34] In other words, baptized Christians are received into full Communion when they are ready. As candidates are discerned to be ready for reception, a Sunday in the near future when the readings of the Mass seem appropriate might be chosen. While the Rite of Reception allows for its celebration to be outside Mass, it makes the most sense to celebrate the rite within Mass, since the culmination of communion and unity would in fact be sharing in the Eucharist.

> The celebration of the sacrament of reconciliation with candidates for reception into full communion is to be carried out at a time prior to and distinct from the celebration of the rite of reception.
>
> *National Statutes for the Catechumenate,* 36

Prior to celebrating this rite, the candidate should celebrate the Sacrament of Penance. Any priest who has the faculty to absolve sins can celebrate this with them.

Celebrating the Rite of Reception

Prior to the Sunday in which reception is celebrated, the assembly may be made aware that a family or individual will be received. The family, as well as the sponsors and companions, may take part in the opening procession with the priest and other ministers. The ministers of hospitality should be alerted to reserve seating for those being received as well as the sponsoring family and companions.

---

33. NS, 33. This seems to conflict with RCIA, 409, located in the chapter "Preparation of Uncatechized Adults for Confirmation and Eucharist": The high point of their entire formation will normally be the Easter Vigil. "At that time they will make a profession of the faith in which they were baptized, receive the sacrament of confirmation, and take part in the Eucharist." It should be noted, however, that this section was originally intended for baptized, uncatechized Catholics.

34. NS, 32.

The Celebration of Reception takes place after the homily. The celebrant invites the candidates forward, the candidates profess their faith, and the celebrant receives the candidates. After the candidates are received, the

celebrant confirms them. The celebrant then takes the hand of the newly received in a gesture of "friendship and acceptance."[35] The Universal Prayer follows the sign of welcome. The congregation may then greet the newly received with a sign of peace after the Universal Prayer, or the sign of peace may be at its usual time prior to Communion.

After receiving the candidate, the celebrant takes her hand in a sign of friendship and acceptance.

If reception is celebrated on a Sunday or solemnity, the readings of the day are used. If it is celebrated on another day, readings may be taken from the day, or from the celebration of reception into full communion, or from the Mass "For Christian Unity." If the Mass is not celebrated at an ordinarily scheduled Sunday Mass, the parish should be invited to participate in the liturgy and a full complement of liturgical ministers, including greeters, music ministers, and trained readers, should serve.

Invitation

After the homily, the celebrant invites the candidate, parent, and sponsor forward. While a text is provided in the rite, the celebrant may also use his own words,[36] which will allow for a certain personalization of the celebration.

Profession of Faith

With the whole liturgical assembly, the candidate recites the Nicene Creed. After the Creed, the candidate alone adds, "I believe and profess all that the holy Catholic Church believes, teaches, and proclaims to be revealed by God." The child may have memorized this, hold a printed copy, or repeat it after the celebrant.

---

35. RCIA, 495.
36. RCIA, 490.

Act of Reception

The celebrant proclaims, "The Lord receives you into the Catholic Church." If Confirmation is not taking place at this liturgy, he lays hands on the candidate's head as he says that. The only reason that Confirmation would not occur is when the person is already validly confirmed, which is the case with those coming from the Orthodox Church and the Old Catholic Church.

Confirmation

The celebrant lays hands over the head of the candidate and prays the prayer of Confirmation. As the sponsor places the right hand on the shoulder of the candidate, the celebrant anoints him or her on the forehead while saying, "N., be sealed with the Gift of the Holy Spirit"; to which the child responds, "Amen." The celebrant then offers the newly confirmed the sign of peace.

The sponsor's right hand is on the candidate's shoulder as the priest anoints him during Confirmation.

Celebrant's Sign of Welcome

Whether Confirmation is celebrated or not, the celebrant offers a sign of welcome, friendship, and acceptance to the newly received. In many parishes the entire assembly offers applause or may even sing a joyful antiphon. Parishes need to take care with the selection of the antiphon to be sure that a sense of triumphalism is not conveyed.

Universal Prayer

At the introduction to the Universal Prayer, the celebrant mentions the initiation sacraments and expresses gratitude to God. At the beginning of the intercessions, the name(s) of the person(s) received is noted. Among the intercessions are prayers for the newly received child and for the unity of the Church.

Sign of Peace

The rite allows for a sign of peace to follow the Universal Prayer, in which the entire assembly greets the newly received. However, since most parishes celebrate the rite of reception at Sunday Mass, the sign of peace would seem best done at its usual place.

Liturgy of the Eucharist

Mass continues with the Liturgy of the Eucharist. The newly received and others may present the gifts of bread and wine. The culmination of reception received into communion and union with the Church is the newly received taking part in Holy Communion for the first time. The newly received and his or her parents and sponsor may receive the Eucharist under both kinds even if this is not the usual practice of the parish.

Recording the Reception

The date of the reception and the sacraments received should be recorded in the parish records, along with the date and place of the child's Baptism.

Frequently Asked Questions

Catechetical Age

1.   What is meant by "children of catechetical age" or "the use of reason"?

In general, the age range for children to participate in the Christian initiation process described in the *Rite of Christian Initiation of Adults* is seven to fourteen years. However, important distinctions need to be made at both ends of the age range. Neither the minimum age of seven nor the maximum age of fourteen is an absolute.

Many in pastoral ministry want to use the age of seven as an absolute: if the child is younger than age seven, she or he is baptized as an infant; seven or older and the child is baptized according to the RCIA. Common sense tells us that it is not quite that black and white. Discernment is needed, as some children younger than the age of seven have the use of reason. The *Code of Canon Law* and the RCIA itself give us guidance.

Canon 11 states "Merely ecclesiastical laws bind those who have been baptized in the Catholic Church or received into it, possess the sufficient use of reason, and, unless the law expressly provides otherwise, have completed seven years of age." The authoritative commentary, *The Code of Canon Law: A Text and Commentary* (James A. Coriden, Thomas J. Green, and Donald E. Heintschel, eds., New York: Paulist Press, 1985) notes that the age of seven is "arbitrary" and that the Church recognizes that "no precise moment can be detected when a child 'receives' the use of reason and begins to make judgments and decisions" (page 32). In addition, the commentary explains that we can presume a child who has completed seven years has sufficient use of reason.[1] This implies that a child younger than age seven could have use of reason, although this is not simply to be presumed. Every child develops differently, and we should respect those differences.

---

1. See also commentary on canon 863 in *New Commentary on the Code of Canon Law*, edited by John P. Beal, James A. Coriden, and Thomas J. Green (New York: Paulist Press, 2000).

In addition, the RCIA gives us a clue as to what is meant by "catecheti-cal age." Paragraph 252 states, "Such children are capable of receiving and nurturing a personal faith and of recognizing an obligation in conscience." Thus, if a child is capable of developing faith, then she or he is old enough for the initiation process. The tricky part is determining if that is the case. By getting to know the child and the parents, one can begin to discern whether the child is capable.

Sometimes the child's capability is obvious, such as when a five- or six-year-old already knows who Jesus is and has faith in God. Some children easily talk about how they pray and tell of stories they know from the Bible.

Pastoral decisions may need to be made at both ends of the age range regarding the ages of "children of catechetical age."

At other times, a child's capability is not as obvious. Discernment does not necessarily occur in one meeting or in one conversation, but as a child participates in the formation pro-cess, an impression of the child's maturity will begin to emerge. Pastoral discretion dictates that it is better to take time to discern rather than to decide what is best for a child based on an arbitrary age.

The same is true for the older end of the age spectrum. Initiation ministers would do well to discern with an adolescent and her or his parents whether the teenager is mature enough to participate in the adult process of initiation (Part I) or whether the ado-lescent is still a child of catechetical age and thus follows Part II, chapter one of the RCIA.

2.   What is the RCIC?

There are two rites of Baptism in the Roman Catholic Church. The *Rite of Baptism for Children* is used for infants and children who have not yet reached the age of reason. The *Rite of Christian Initiation of Adults* (RCIA) describes the steps and the stages leading to the sacraments of initiation for adults, including children who have reached the age of reason. The RCIA includes the chapter "Christian Initiation of Children Who Have Reached Catechetical Age," which offers ways that the steps and the stages may be accommodated for children. There is no RCIC because there is no Rite of Christian Initiation of Children.

3. At what age is parental permission required for initiation?

Parental permission is required for children of catechetical age to be initiated.[2] At what age, then, is an adolescent no longer a child of catechetical age? John M. Huels points out that "the law gives no upper age limit on those who are considered children of catechetical age" (John M. Huels, *The Catechumenate and the Law: A Pastoral and Canonical Commentary for the Church in the United States* [Chicago: Liturgy Training Publications, 1994], 25).

The reason that fourteen years is often given as the upper age limit for participating in Christian initiation accommodated to children of catechetical age is that canon 863 states, "The baptism of adults, at least of those who have completed their fourteenth year, is to be deferred to the diocesan bishop."

Nonetheless, adolescents who are fourteen years old are still dependent on their parents or guardians. Canon 97 §1 recognizes that those under eighteen years of age are minors. Pastoral ministers should seek parental permission for anyone who is under the age of eighteen.

Moreover, adolescents who are fifteen, sixteen, or seventeen years old are not well served by being with adults in the catechumenate. At the same time, they are likely too old for the children's catechumenate. Thus, special adaptations must be made for adolescents. Their same-age companions can assist them throughout the initiation process and some of the catechesis for the Sacrament of Confirmation may be appropriate for teen catechumens.[3]

4. Must parents be involved when children participate in the catechumenate? Can a child become Catholic if the parents are not Catholic or not even Christian? Can someone else stand in for a parent?

If the parents give their permission and the child has sufficient desire and intention to receive the sacraments, she or he can be received into the Church. However, pastoral ministers must consider the wisdom of initiating a child into the faith if there is little support at home for practice of the faith.

---

2. RCIA, 252, 254.
3. NS, 19.

Ideally, parents should be involved when a child seeks initiation. Permission is the minimum required from the parents, but it is desirable that their participation be much more than that. The Church sees parents as integral to the process. Indeed, the children's formation "depends on" the "influence of their parents."[4] Parents accompany, support, and guide their children throughout the journey of initiation.

There are, however, any number of circumstances when parents cannot be involved. The RCIA addresses this issue, stating that when parents cannot be present, their place should be taken by sponsors.[5] Although paragraph 260 is referring to a sponsor's role in the Rite of Acceptance, this also applies to the broader initiation process. If a parent or guardian cannot be involved or refuses to be involved, a parish sponsor can accompany the child throughout the process, although the parent still must grant permission.

There is an additional benefit to having a parish sponsor. If the parish sponsor is a parent with baptized children of catechetical age, the children in the sponsoring family serve as companions to the children seeking initiation. In this way, the entire Catholic family serves as a sponsor to the catechumenal family.

A sponsoring family can be beneficial even when the parents are involved. It is often the case that parents in the catechumenal family have themselves been away from the Church, or that they are new to the parish, or are themselves candidates for initiation. The sponsoring family not only accompanies the child; the sponsoring family also supports, guides, and assists the parents.

5. Can a parent compel a child of catechetical age to go through the initiation process and be baptized?

A child of catechetical age, who has the use of reason, is considered an adult for purposes of initiation.[6] Canon 865 §1 states, "For an adult to be baptized, the person must have manifested the intention to receive baptism." If a child does not want to join the Church, it would seem that the necessary intention is not present for Baptism.

---

4. RCIA, 254.

5. RCIA, 260.

6. CIC, c. 852 §1.

6. Can a child with special needs go through the catechumenal process?

As with all children, discernment with the parents and initiation minister is important. A child who is capable of forming a personal faith should be helped to do so according to his or her age and capacity. The method of catechesis, the participation in various rites, and the occasion for celebrating the sacraments of initiation should be decided according to the needs and sensitivities of the child and family.

Children with special needs who have not attained the use of reason, no matter what their age, are considered children for purposes of initiation and are baptized, at the request of the parents, with the *Rite of Baptism for Children*.

7. Should baptized children receive the Sacrament of Penance for the first time during the Penitential Rites (Scrutinies) with the children preparing for initiation?

Although it is worthy to have baptized children of the catechetical group celebrate with the unbaptized as members of the worshipping assembly, it is disconcerting to combine the Sacrament of Penance with a Scrutiny. We turn to the adult rite for an answer. For adults, there is no corresponding Lenten penitential rite in which the unbaptized and baptized are combined. In fact, in paragraph 463, there is a directive to avoid combining the baptized with the unbaptized for Penitential Rites (Scrutinies) for adults preparing for Confirmation and Eucharist. Follow Part I instead.

Order of the Sacraments

1. Why don't we just baptize the children and let them catch up with their classmates and receive the sacraments when they do?

First among the reasons we initiate children of catechetical age the way we do is the Paschal Mystery, the Passion, Death, and Resurrection of Jesus Christ. The Paschal Mystery is the core of our faith as Christians. If a child is old enough to grasp even the smallest part of this saving mystery, we want to share it with them. And, the best way to share it is for them to enter into it through the Sacraments of Baptism, Confirmation, and Eucharist.

We celebrate the full outpouring of God's grace in the sacraments of initiation. Through these sacraments the Holy Spirit incorporates the children into Christ, who is priest, prophet, and king. If the children have the

use of reason, why would we withhold a portion of sacramental grace? Catching up with Catholic peers is not a sufficient reason to delay the Sacrament of Confirmation. Regarding the reception of Baptism and Confirmation, paragraph 215 of the rite states (remember that for purposes of initiation, "adult" means anyone who has reached the age of reason):

When we allow children to enter into all of the sacraments of initiation, we are sharing the core of our faith, the Paschal Mystery, with them.

Adults are not to be baptized without receiving confirmation immediately afterward, unless some serious reason stands in the way. The conjunction of the two celebrations signifies the unity of the paschal mystery, the close link between the mission of the Son and the outpouring of the Holy Spirit, and the connection between the two sacraments through which the Son and the Holy Spirit come with the Father to those who are baptized.

Similarly, the *Code of Canon Law* highlights the importance of the unity of the sacraments of initiation in canon 842 §2, which states, "The sacraments of baptism, confirmation, and the Most Holy Eucharist are interrelated in such a way that they are required for full Christian initiation," and in canon 866: "Unless there is a grave reason to the contrary, an adult who is baptized is to be confirmed immediately after baptism and is to participate in the eucharistic celebration also by receiving communion."

There is no law or rule in the Church that states that all children have to receive sacraments in the same way or at the same time. Indeed, the Church has two traditions. Those baptized as infants with the *Rite of Baptism for Children* celebrate Confirmation and Eucharist when they reach the age of reason. Those baptized when they have the use of reason follow the *Rite of Christian Initiation of Adults*, receiving the three sacraments of initiation in the same celebration.

The following is a list of useful references that pertain to the unity of the sacraments of initiation with children of catechetical age from the *Rite of Christian Initiation of Adults*: paragraphs 14, 215, 304, 305, 308, 323, and

329; from the *National Statutes for the United States*: statutes 14, 18, and 19; from the *Code of Canon Law*: canons 842, 852, 866, 883, and 885.

2. If children receive all three sacraments of initiation, will they come back? Will we lose them?

If the process of initiation has truly been a journey of conversion, then the children will return for continuing religious formation. If they developed a relationship with Jesus Christ and the Christian community, then they will come back. They will want to return. They will want to continue to grow, learn, and deepen their relationship with Christ.

Good mystagogy for the children is important. And, most important, the parish must have well-celebrated worship, quality religious education, and genuine community in Christ to nourish and sustain the neophytes. The responsibility belongs to the whole parish.

Combining Children and Adults

1. Do adults and children celebrate the rites together?

For children the rites are essential to the process and "as with adults" are to mark the steps in the initiation process.[7] In Part II, chapter one, the ritual text provides liturgical rites specially designed for children. The liturgical rites given for children are the

- Rite of Acceptance into the Order of Catechumens (260–276);
- Optional Rite of Election (277–290);
- Penitential Rites or Scrutinies (291–303); and
- Sacraments of Initiation (304–329).

The rites listed are to be celebrated with children only, but in many parishes both adults and children are in the initiation process. Celebrating a ritual with adults and children in the same celebration is an effective adaptation of the separate rites given in the ritual text. Although the adult rites are in Part I and the children's rites are in Part II, a careful combination of the two makes for a celebration that reflects the face of the parish. Furthermore, combining adults and children in the same celebration is vital when a parent and child in the same family are being initiated.

---

7. RCIA, 253.

Particular questions arise with the Penitential Rites or Scrutinies for children. Initiation ministers often wonder why only one Penitential Rite (Scrutiny) is given when three are provided for adults.

At first read, the rite looks difficult to execute. A closer reading of the ritual text can eliminate the problem. The first paragraph describing the Scrutinies with children[8] advises us to follow and adapt "the adult rite (nos. 141–146) . . . since the children's penitential rites have a similar purpose." This is a good general principle to follow whenever one has questions. When in doubt, follow Part I.

Celebrating a ritual with adults and children in the same celebration is an effective adaptation of the separate rites.

Moreover, paragraph 294 makes a similar point by telling us that when celebrating a second Scrutiny with children, "the texts for the intercessions and prayer of exorcism given in the adult rite (nos. 153–154, 167–168, 174–175) are used, with requisite modifications." Overall, it is advisable to use the three Scrutinies in Part I with unbaptized children, particularly when adults are also celebrating the Scrutinies. It is not necessary to celebrate separate Scrutinies with children.

Do not overlook rites with children during any part of the process. The children will benefit from the minor rites of the catechumenate in Part I.[9] The rituals of the catechumenate are appropriate and formative for children as well as adults. Take full advantage of the Celebrations of the Word, Blessings, Exorcisms, and Anointings that are given for the benefit of catechumens.

8. RCIA, 291.
9. RCIA, 81–105.

2. Do we combine children's catechumenal sessions with those for the adults, or should the sessions be separate?

At times it is appropriate and effective to combine catechumenal sessions for children and adults, and at other times, it is best for sessions to be separate. Several factors help to determine the best approach.

Consider the ages of the children and whether parents are also candidates for initiation. When children and parents from the same family are candidates for initiation, especially beneficial is a family-centered process in which parents and children journey together. Plus, such a process provides an easier schedule for parents.

When children and adults are together, intergenerational sessions are designed so they benefit all participants, not just families with children. Obviously, certain instructional parts of a session are done separately. During an intergenerational session, children and adults often separate for parts of the session into age-appropriate groups. For example, a session might start with an introduction and prayer, split into age groups for topical catechesis, and come back together to close with one of the minor rites of the catechumenate.

Similarly, certain elements of catechumenal formation are best done separately, whereas other elements might be better together. Dismissal catechesis during the Period of the Catechumenate is usually done with children and adults in separate sessions, but the number and ages of the catechumens may affect that determination. When adults and children celebrate the liturgical rites together, they are also with each other as they prepare for and reflect on the rite afterwards.

Follow the wisdom offered in paragraph 76 of the RCIA: "Nothing, therefore, can be settled a priori." And, as experienced initiation ministers are fond of saying, "Adapt, adapt, adapt."[10] What works one year for one group of catechumens may not work the next year. Or, it may work in one parish, but not in another. Let the Holy Spirit be the guide.

---

10. See RCIA, 35.

Baptism

1. What if the Catholic Church does not recognize as valid the baptism of someone seeking to be received into the Catholic Church?

If the Catholic Church does not recognize the validity of the baptism of the child who has come seeking membership, that person is treated canonically as a catechumen. Care must be taken to explain the situation to the child's family and to deal with it pastorally. If the child is well catechized in the Christian faith, an abbreviated catechumenate may be appropriate. If a festive celebration of Baptism would be a source of discord to the family, a simpler celebration might be considered.

2. How does one prove that he or she was baptized?

The usual way to prove that one is baptized is by the presentation of a certificate or letter from the community at which the Baptism took place. In the absence of such proof, the testimony of a parent or other person who was present at the event may suffice, or even the testimony of the person, if they were old enough to remember and can recall the event sufficiently. Other evidence such as photos, a record in a family Bible, or an inscription in a gift or card given at the time may serve. As a last resort, the person may need to be baptized conditionally in a private setting.

Confirmation

1. Who is to be confirmed when baptized and received into the Church?

Adults and children who have reached catechetical age are to be confirmed at the same liturgy at which they are baptized.[11] The Confirmation of a child of catechetical age is not to be delayed so that the child can be confirmed with his or her class. When the time comes, such children can certainly participate in the catechesis for Confirmation with their classmates. In some dioceses, the bishops recognize and bless these children at the parish celebration of Confirmation.

---

11. RCIA, 215; CIC, c. 866 NS, 18–19.

When baptized candidates are received into the full communion of the Roman Catholic Church they are to be confirmed at the time of their profession of faith and reception. Their Confirmation is not to be deferred.[12]

2. Who has the responsibility to confirm?

The diocesan bishop is the ordinary minister of the sacraments of initiation for adults. However, any priest who baptizes someone of catechetical age or older, or receives someone into the full communion of the Catholic Church, by law has the responsibility to confirm this person.[13]

Priests who do not exercise a pastoral office but participate in a catechumenate require a mandate from the diocesan bishop if they are to baptize; they do not require any additional mandate or authorization in order to confirm but have the faculty to confirm from the law, as do priests who baptize in the exercise of the pastoral office.[14]

3. Is it permissible at one celebration for one priest to baptize and another to confirm?

No. The faculty to confirm is only granted to the one who baptizes. If there are a large number to be confirmed, the presiding minister may invite other priests to assist him in the anointing according the norms prescribed in RCIA, 14.

4. Can a priest confirm a baptized Catholic?

A priest who wishes to confirm a baptized Catholic outside of the norms of the RCIA explicitly request this faculty from the diocesan bishop.[15] The only exception is in the case of a baptized Catholic who, through no fault of their own, has been instructed in a non-Catholic religion or in the case of the readmission to communion of a baptized Catholic who has been an apostate from the faith.[16]

---

12. NS, 35; CIC, c. 885 §1.
13. CIC, cc. 883 2°, 885 §2.
14. NS, 12.
15. CIC, c. 884 §1.
16. NS, 28, 29.

5. If candidates who are received into full communion
    have already been confirmed in the community where
    they were baptized, should they still be confirmed?

The Roman Catholic Church accepts the Confirmation of only the Orthodox
Church and the Old Catholic Church. All others need to be confirmed in the
Roman Catholic Church. If there is doubt, pastoral ministers should consult
with their chancery.

Parish, School Involvement

1. Do children in the catechumenal process also
    participate in the regular religious-education program?

Sometimes. It depends on the needs of the child. There are pros and cons to
an unbaptized and/or uncatechized child participating in a religious-education
program that is designed for baptized, catechized children.

Participation in the parish religious-education program can help the
child preparing for initiation connect with their Catholic peers. Getting to
know other children in the parish will help them make friends and become
a part of the larger community.

RCIA, 254, stresses the importance of the relationship between the
children seeking initiation and the "children of the same age who are already
baptized and are preparing for confirmation and eucharist." It goes on to say
that "their initiation progresses gradually and within the supportive setting
of this group of companions."[17] In other words, the baptized children of the
parish accompany the unbaptized children on their journey of initiation. The
Catholic children in the parish are the companions for children who want
to become Catholic. When inquirers or catechumens are part of the parish
religious-education program, these relationships may naturally develop.

Sharing catechesis is certainly another advantage to having these children participate in the regular catechetical program. Children seeking initiation are catechized along with their Catholic peers. They learn the doctrines,
prayers, and traditions of the Church in the midst of their same-age companions. *National Statutes*, 19, also speaks of the sharing of "some elements of
ordinary catechetical instruction" of the baptized with the unbaptized.

---

17. RCIA, 254.1.

But this seeming benefit can also be a disadvantage. Some children in the initiation process have not yet been evangelized and thus are not yet ready for a formal and systematic catechesis that is geared toward baptized children. The *General Directory for Catechesis* (GDC) reminds us that the Church desires that "the first stage in the catechetical process be dedicated to ensuring conversion."[18] Furthermore, a "pre-catechesis" is necessary for catechesis to take root in the heart.[19]

Thus, we must assess whether the child has been evangelized before automatically putting her or him into a formal religious-education class. It may be fine for some children, but depending upon the age, background, and personality of the child, it can be overwhelming and discouraging to be in a class with unfamiliar material and individuals. Sometimes the class is discussing subject matter that is foreign to an inquirer or a catechumen.

Therefore, discernment is necessary before routinely placing children preparing for initiation in the religious-education program. Sometimes younger children particularly assimilate easily into a Catholic classroom setting. At other times, the religious-education classroom can be uncomfortable for a child in the catechumenate, particularly in later elementary or middle school when catechists, classmates, and textbooks presume a certain level of knowledge. Discussion with the child and the parent or guardian about what best fits the needs of the child and the family is the best way to decide this question.

2. What is the role of the Catholic school in Christian initiation with children?

Many children and adolescents seek initiation via the Catholic school. They are evangelized by their classmates, teachers, parents, coaches, and the entire Christian community associated with the school. Often, it is the school community that provides the ready-made "supportive setting" that is described in RCIA, 254 §1. Religion classes taught in the school provide some of the catechesis that is necessary for their formation in "the Christian way of life."[20]

At the same time, it is extremely important that initiation is grounded in a parish community that celebrates Eucharist every Sunday. Those who seek initiation must be connected to a parish in addition to the school. This

---

18. GDC, 62.
19. GDC, 62.
20. RCIA, 75 §2.

Peers in Catholic school often give young catechumens needed support.

is important because the parish is the locus of Sunday Eucharist. Families with children preparing for initiation must be connected to a community that celebrates Eucharist every Sunday because the Eucharist is the source and summit of the Christian life. The Sunday Eucharist is the community's preeminent celebration of the Paschal Mystery. And, the Paschal Mystery is the heart of initiation.[21] It is at the parish liturgies that the rites occur and where the children will be baptized and will continue to celebrate the Eucharist after their initiation. Classmates of the children preparing for Baptism should be encouraged to be present when catechumenal rites are taking place and to participate in the celebration of the sacraments of initiation.

3. How is the whole parish involved in Christian initiation?

The main way that parishioners participate in Christian initiation is by their presence and participation. The joyful participation of the faithful in the rites of the catechumenal process is felt and appreciated. When there are opportunities to greet the catechumens, either at the church or in the community, parishioners should offer a welcoming word. As members of the parish become aware of the names of the catechumens, they should include them in their prayers.

---

21. RCIA, 8.

Reception into Full Communion

1. How are baptized children below the age of reason received into the full communion of the Catholic Church?

Nothing is required of children validly baptized and below the age of reason when they are received into the full communion of the Catholic Church at the time one or both parents is received or at another time at the request of the Catholic parent. Their original Baptism, however, ought to be carefully recorded into the baptismal register with a note of their becoming Catholic through their parents' initiation or request. It is presumed that they would be confirmed and would receive Eucharist along with the other children of the parish at the customary times.

2. Are baptized but uncatechized candidates for reception into the full communion of the Roman Catholic Church obligated to celebrate the Sacrament of Reconciliation prior to their profession of faith?

RCIA, 482, states, "If the profession of faith and reception into the full communion takes place within Mass, the candidate, according to his or her own conscience, should make a confession of sins beforehand, first informing the confessor that he or she is about to be received into full communion."

Recording the Sacraments

1. Where are the names of catechumens recorded after the Rite of Acceptance into the Order of Catechumens is celebrated?

Because the catechumens are joined to the Church and are part of the household of Christ,[22] their status is taken seriously. Their names should be recorded in the parish register of catechumens, along with the names of the sponsors and the minister and the date and place of the celebration.[23]

---

22. RCIA, 47.
23. RCIA, 46.

2. Where are the names of the neophytes recorded after the sacraments of initiation are celebrated?

Their names are recorded in the parish baptismal register. Notations are recorded in the Confirmation register, and also in the Communion register.

3. Where are the names of the baptized Christians who enter into the full communion of the Roman Catholic Church recorded?

The name of the person received into full communion with the Catholic Church by means of a profession of faith is to be recorded in the parish register under the date of profession together with the date and place of the Baptism of the party, along with the other information required for the baptismal register. If the parish maintains a profession of faith register, the name of the person is also recorded in it.

Information is also recorded in the Confirmation and Communion registers.

RESOURCES

Church Documents

- *General Directory for Catechesis* Promulgated in 1997, from the Congregation for Clergy, this is the Catholic Church's guide to catechizing on the teachings of the Church. It is directed mainly at bishops and those preparing catechisms and other materials for pastoral use.

- *National Directory for Catechesis.* Washington, DC: United States Conference of Catholic Bishops, 2005. Based on the *General Directory for Catechesis* (GDC), this resource seeks to be a pastoral tool more than the *General Directory for Catechesis.* It builds on some of the core themes of the GDC, like the relationship of catechesis to evangelization and worship, and provides practical tools for doing catechesis.

- *Rite of Baptism for Children.* Washington, DC: United States Conference of Catholic Bishops, 1970. This is the Roman Catholic ritual for baptizing those who have not yet reached the age of reason.

- *Rite of Christian Initiation of Adults.* Chicago: Liturgy Training Publications, 1988. This is the Roman Catholic ritual for initiating those who have reached the age of reason, with directives for preparing adults and children of catechetical age for the sacraments of initiation. This is the basic guide for anyone directing Christian initiation in a ministerial setting.

- *Rito de iniciación cristiana de adultos.* Washington, DC: United States Conference of Catholic Bishops, 1991; copublished by The Liturgical Press, Collegeville, MN, and Liturgy Training Publications, Chicago. Spanish edition of the *Rite of Christian Initiation of Adults* for use in the dioceses of the United States of America.

Pastoral Resources

- Clay, Michael. *A Harvest for God: Christian Initiation in the Rural and Small-Town Parish.* Chicago: Liturgy Training Publications, 2003. This book is designed to help implement the RCIA in a way appropriate to the situation and culture of rural and small-town parishes. It is useful for any parish with limited people and resources.

- Galipeau, Jerry. *Apprenticed to Christ Activities for Practicing the Catholic Way of Life.* Franklin Park, IL: World Library Publications, 2007. This book offers suggested ways those in the process of initiation can be integrated into the life of the parish, making use of the various ministries, outreaches, and activities already established in the parish. This collection of activities is rooted in RCIA, 75, and is geared toward the Sundays of the liturgical year.

- Huck, Gabe. *The Three Days: Parish Prayer in the Paschal Triduum,* Revised. Chicago: Liturgy Training Publications, 1992. This is a thorough exploration of all the moments that make up the great Paschal Triduum. It provides a solid theology and spirituality of the three-day feast, as it can be lived out in a parish setting. This approach gives a solid context for the parish's initiation ministry to see and understand its place in the observance of these most holy days.

- Huels, John M. *The Catechumenate and the Law: A Pastoral and Canonical Commentary for the Church in the United States.* Chicago: Liturgy Training Publications, 2003, 1994. As a rite of the Church, the RCIA is a canonical document as well as a liturgical one. This eminent canonist examines how the law affects persons (candidates, catechumens, ministers, children, sponsors, and godparents) and situations (invalid or doubtful Baptism and Confirmations, marriage cases, delaying Confirmation, and record keeping), offering pastoral and canonical guidance.

- Kavanagh, Aidan. *The Shape of Baptism: The Rite of Christian Initiation.* Collegeville, MN: Pueblo Publishing Company, Inc., 1978. This theological and pastoral commentary provides practical analysis of Christian initiation within the Roman Rite.

- Lewinski, Ron. *Guide for Sponsors,* Fourth Edition. Chicago: Liturgy Training Publications, 2008. Anyone who has been asked to sponsor an individual who is becoming Catholic will find support in this book.

The resource provides an understanding of the *Rite of Christian Initiation of Adults* as it introduces a mentor in the faith to ways to accompany a catechumen. The chapter "Frequently Asked Questions" addresses many concerns that sponsors have.

- Lewinski, Ron. *Manual para Padrinas y Madrinas de Catecúmenos.* Chicago: Liturgy Training Publications, 2008. The Spanish translation of *Guide for Sponsors* will provide assistance in Spanish-speaking communities.

- Lewinski, Ron. *Welcoming the New Catholic.* Third Edition. Chicago: Liturgy Training Publications, 1993. This is a thorough, basic introduction to the catechumenal process. It begins with stating a pastoral approach to ministering to those desiring to become members of the Church and describes the steps and stages outlined in the RCIA with that approach in mind.

- McMahon, Michael J. *The Rite of Christian Initiation of Adults: A Pastoral Liturgical Commentary.* Revised edition. Washington, DC: Federation of Diocesan Liturgical Commissions, 2002. This study guide presents documentation from the RCIA and other pertinent Church documents, commentary, and study questions for every aspect of the initiation of adults,

- Metzdorff, Jo-Ann and Paul Turner, *Guide for Celebrating First Communion.* Chicago: Liturgy Training Publications, 2015. This book is not primarily about children in the catechumenal process, but it contains much that is of interest to anyone who deals with baptized children preparing for sacraments, particularly those preparing for the Sacrament of Penance.

- Miller, Janet. *Friends on the Way: Children's Catechumenate Resource.* TeamRCIA.com.

- This is a catechetical resource for children in the catechumenate period of RCIA. There is a dismissal session and catechetical session for each Sunday of the liturgical year. There are clear directions for catechists and intergenerational activities included for parents of the child catechumens. This is an e-resource that can be downloaded and used repeatedly.

- Mitchell, Nathan. *Forum Essays: Eucharist as Sacrament of Initiation.* Chicago: Liturgy Training Publications, 1994. In three essays, Mitchell considers the Eucharist as the act that completes the sacraments of initiation. The chapters examine the path taken to come to the table of the Lord, the meaning of Jesus' inclusiveness while dining with others, and recognizing the mystery of the Body of Christ within those who receive the Eucharist.

- Morris, Thomas H. *The RCIA: Transforming the Church; A Resource for Pastoral Implementation.* Revised and updated edition. New York: Paulist Press, 1997. If every RCIA minister is to have the *Rite of Christian Initiation of Adults* in one hand, Morris' book in the other hand is appropriate. This is an excellent resource that takes the vision of the RCIA and shows how that vision can take shape in the parish setting.

- Nye, Rebecca. *Children's Spirituality: What it is and Why it Matters.* London: Church House Publishing, 2009. This book is a simple, practical introduction to children's spirituality. The reader is invited to reflect upon her or his spirituality as a way of recognizing the importance of childhood spirituality. Principles for nurturing children's spirituality are given. The author, Dr. Rebecca Nye, is a proponent of "Godly Play," an innovative approach to Christian religious education. Dr. Nye is originally a psychologist and has held research posts at Nottingham and Cambridge Universities in the United Kingdom.

- O'Connor, Francine M. *Journey of Faith for Children.* Ligouri, MO: Liguori Publications, 1998. These topical handouts are designed for the various periods of the RCIA. Each handout provides scriptural references and thought-provoking questions that can be used as support material.

- Paprocki, Joe, and D. Todd Williamson. *Great is the Mystery: The Formational Power of Liturgy.* Chicago: Liturgy Training Publications, 2012. This book walks through the foundational principles of Catholic liturgical life and breaks them open, making them accessible and understandable. It explores the various elements and dynamics of liturgical spirituality, an understanding of liturgy, the liturgical year, and an in-depth look at each part of the weekly celebration of the parish Eucharist.

- Repp, Debbie. *Journey of Faith for Teens.* Ligouri, MO: Liguori Publications, 2005. These topical handouts are designed for the various periods of the catechumenal process. Each handout provides scriptural references and thought-provoking questions that can be used as support material.

- Senseman, Rita Burns. *A Child's Journey: The Christian Initiation of Children*. Cincinnati, OH: St. Anthony Messenger Press, 1998. TeamRCIA.com. This book examines the many issues that arise with the initiation of children and offers practical approaches for dealing with those issues.

- Senseman, Rita Burns. *Teens in the RCIA: A Journey of Conversion.* TeamRCIA.com. This downloadable resource offers solid information for adapting the Christian initiation process for younger and older teens, using what is most applicable to each group from what the RCIA says about initiating adults and children.

- Tufano, Victoria M., Paul Turner, and D. Todd Williamson. *Guide for Celebrating Christian Initiation with Adults.* Chicago: Liturgy Training Publications, 2016. After exploring the theological and historical developments of Christian initiation, the authors guide the readers through the celebration of the rites during each period and step of the *Rite of Christian Initiation of Adults.* The resource provides additional materials on the initiation process and answers queries about the RCIA.

- Tufano, Victoria M., ed. *Readings in the Christian Initiation of Children*, Chicago: Liturgy Training Publications, 1994. This collection of articles first published in *Catechumenate: A Journal of Christian Initiation*, examines the issues of initiating children from the theoretical to the practical.

- Turner, Paul. *Guide for Celebrating Confirmation.* Chicago: Liturgy Training Publications, 2016. This book focuses on preparations for Confirmation but will be of interest to those involved in the RCIA. It provides more material on the theological and historical developments of Confirmation and answers questions about the sacrament.

- Vincie, Catherine. *Forum Essays: The Role of the Assembly in Christian Initiation*. Chicago: Liturgy Training Publications, 1993. Examines the ritual texts of the *Rite of Christian Initiation of Adults* and the reform of the rites and their implementation in parishes in light of the *Constitution on the Sacred Liturgy's* stance that all members of the assembly have a role in the liturgy.

- Wagner, Nick. *The Way of Faith: A Field Guide for the RCIA Process.* Twenty-Third Publications, 2008. This book offers a solid overview of the process of initiation as it can be implemented in the parish setting. Wagner does an excellent job of addressing each of the periods of the initiation process and addressing the who, what, where, when, why, and how of each period.

- *Young Apprentices.* rclbyoungapprentices.com. This is an online subscription resource for catechumenate directors and catechists who work with children and youth in the catechumenal process.

Academic Resources

- Beal, James. James Coriden, and Thomas J. Green. *New Commentary on the Code of Canon Law.* New York: Paulist Press, 2000. The new comprehensive scholarly commentary on the *Code of Canon Law* includes a revised English translation of the Code and reflects developments in canon law since the original commentary was published.

- Coriden, James A., Thomas J. Green and Donald E. Heintschel, eds. *The Code of Canon Law: A Text and Commentary*, New York: Paulist Press, 1985. A thorough scholarly commentary on every section of the Code of Canon Law.

GLOSSARY

Adult: For the purpose of sacramental initiation, a person who has reached the age of reason (also called the age of discretion or catechetical age), usually regarded to be seven years of age, is an adult. A person who has reached that age is to be initiated into the Church according to the *Rite of Christian Initiation of Adults* and receive the three sacraments of initiation together, although the catechesis should be adapted to the individual's needs. Before this age, the person is considered an infant and is baptized using the *Rite of Baptism for Children.*

Apostles' Creed: The ancient baptismal statement of the Church's faith. The questions used in the celebration of Baptism correspond to the statements of the Apostles' Creed.

Baptismal font: The pool or basin at which the Sacrament of Baptism is administered.

Blessing: Any prayer that praises and thanks God. In particular, *blessing* describes those prayers in which God is praised because of some person or object, and thus the individual or object is seen to have become specially dedicated or sanctified because of the prayer of faith.

Book of the Elect: A book into which the names of those catechumens who have been chosen, or elected, for initiation at the next Easter Vigil, are written at or before the Rite of Election.

Book of the Gospels: A ritual book from which the passages from the accounts of the Gospel prescribed for Masses on Sundays, solemnities, feasts of the Lord and of the saints, and ritual Masses are proclaimed; also called an evangeliary.

Candidate: In its broadest definition, the term refers to anyone preparing to receive a sacrament. In the *Rite of Christian Initiation of Adults,* the term is used as a general designation for adults who are expressing an interest in the Catholic faith, whether baptized or not. In common usage, *candidate* is used for a baptized person preparing for reception into the full communion of the Catholic Church; an unbaptized person inquiring about preparing for Christian initiation is called an inquirer.

Catechesis: Instruction and spiritual formation in the faith, teachings, and traditions of the Church.

Catechetical age: Usually considered to be about seven years of age; also called the age of reason or the age of discretion. For the purpose of Christian initiation, a person who has reached catechetical age is considered an adult and is to be initiated into the Church according to the *Rite of Christian Initiation of Adults.*

Catechumen: An unbaptized person who has declared his or her intention to prepare for the sacraments of initiation and has been accepted into the Order of Catechumens. Catechumens, though not yet fully initiated, are joined to the Church and are considered part of the household of Christ.

Catechumenate: The second of four periods in the process of Christian initiation as described in the *Rite of Christian Initiation of Adults.* The period begins with the Rite of Acceptance into the Order of Catechumens. It is a period of nurturing and growth of the catechumens' faith and conversion to God in Christ. Sometimes the term *catechumenate* is used to refer to the entire initiation process.

Celebrant: The presiding minister at worship.

Child: For the purposes of Christian initiation, one who has not yet reached the age of discernment (age of reason, presumed to be about seven years of age) and therefore cannot profess personal faith.

Chrism: One of the three Holy Oils. It is consecrated by the bishop at the Chrism Mass and used at the Baptism of infants, at Confirmation, at the ordination of priests and bishops, and at the dedication of churches and altars. Chrism is scented, usually with balsam.

Companion: In the Christian initiation process with children of catechetical age, a baptized child of an age similar to the child catechumen who takes part in the catechetical group and accompanies the catechumen in the rites.

Confirmation: The sacrament that continues the initiation process begun in Baptism and marks the sealing of the Holy Spirit. It is administered through an anointing with chrism on the forehead with the words, "*N.*, be sealed with the Gift of the Holy Spirit," preceded by the imposition of hands.

Dismissal: The final, formal invitation by the deacon or, in his absence, the priest for the assembly to go forth from the liturgical celebration. The word can also refer to the dismissal of the catechumens after the homily at Mass.

Easter Vigil: The liturgy celebrated during the night before Easter Sunday; it begins after nightfall and ends before daybreak on Sunday. While the Church keeps watch this night, a fire is lighted, Scriptures are read that tell the story of salvation, the elect receive the Easter sacraments, and all present renew their baptismal promises.

Elect: Catechumens who have been formally called, or elected, by the Church for Baptism, Confirmation, and Eucharist at the next Easter Vigil.

***Ephphetha* Rite:** A rite of opening the ears and the mouth, associated with the celebration of Baptism. The rite, which has its origin in Mark 7:31–37, Jesus' healing of a deaf man, prays that the one being baptized may hear and profess the faith. It may be performed with the elect as part of their preparation on Holy Saturday for initiation at the Easter Vigil or as part of the *Rite of Baptism for Children*.

Evangelization: The continuing mission of the Church to spread the Gospel of Jesus Christ to all people. The Period of Evangelization and Precatechumenate includes the invitation, the welcoming, the witness, the sharing of faith, and the proclamation of the Gospel to inquirers.

Exorcism: A prayer or command given to cast out the presence of the devil. The *Rite of Baptism for Children* contains a prayer of exorcism; the *Rite of Christian Initiation of Adults* contains prayers of exorcism as part of the rites belonging to the Period of the Catechumenate and as part of the Scrutinies. There is a *Rite of Exorcism* for use in the case of possession; it may be used only with the express permission of a bishop and only by mandated priest-exorcists.

Faculty: A right granted to enable a person to do something, usually referring to a right granted to a priest or deacon by law or by the bishop.

Godparents: Members of the Christian community, chosen for their good example and their close relationship to the one being baptized, who are present at the celebration of Baptism and provide guidance and assistance to the one baptized afterward.

Holy Saturday: The Saturday within the Sacred Paschal Triduum. It is a day marked by meditation, prayer, and fasting in anticipation of the Resurrection of the Lord. Several Preparation Rites for the elect who will be receiving the sacraments of initiation at the Vigil are proper to this day.

Immersion: A method of Baptism in which the candidate is submerged either entirely or partially in the baptismal water.

Infusion: A method of Baptism in which the baptismal water is poured over the head of the candidate.

Inquirer: An unbaptized adult who is in the very first stage of the process of Christian initiation.

Inquiry: Another name given to the period of evangelization and precatechumenate, the first period or stage in the process of Christian initiation.

Initiation: The process by which a person enters the faith life of the Church—from the catechumenate through the normally continuous celebration of the entrance rites of Baptism, Confirmation, and the Eucharist.

Laying on of hands: A gesture of blessing or invocation recorded in the New Testament in conjunction with prayer (for example, Acts 13:3; 2 Timothy 1:6). The gesture is performed by extending both hands forward with the palms turned downward. Depending on the circumstances, the hands may be placed on the person's head or stretched out over a group of people or over an object.

Litany of the Saints: A litany that calls upon the saints to pray for the Church, believed to be the most ancient litany in the Church's worship.

Minor rites: Rites during the catechumenate, which include the Rite of Exorcism, Rite of Blessing, and Rite of Anointing.

Mystagogy: The postbaptismal catechesis given to the newly baptized during Easter Time, wherein the neophyte and the local Church share the meaning of the initiatory mysteries and experience.

National Statutes for the Catechumenate: A document issued by the United States Bishops in 1986, and confirmed by the Apostolic See in 1988, constituting particular law for the implementation of the RCIA in the United States.

Neophyte: One who is recently initiated. It comes from the word meaning *new plant* or *twig, a new sprout on a branch.* After the Period of Mystagogy the new Catholic is no longer called neophyte.

Oil of Catechumens: The oil, blessed by the bishop at the Chrism Mass (or for pastoral reasons by the priest before the anointing) to be used in the anointing of the catechumens during the process of initiation.

Order of Catechumens: The canonical group to which an unbaptized adult who is preparing to receive the sacraments of initiation belongs after celebrating the *Rite of Acceptance into the Order of Catechumens.*

Paschal Mystery: The saving mystery of Christ's Passion, Death, and Resurrection. It is the mystery that is celebrated and made present in every liturgy, and the mystery that every Christian is to imitate and be united with in everyday life.

Penance: The sacrament by which the baptized, through the mercy of God, receive pardon for their sins and reconciliation with the Church. This sacrament is most commonly celebrated by the private confession of sin and expression of sorrow by a penitent to a confessor, who then offers absolution. It is also commonly called confession or the Sacrament of Reconciliation.

Postbaptismal catechesis: Mystagogical catechesis, instruction given to the newly baptized, or neophytes, to help them deepen their understanding of the faith primarily through reflection on the sacraments they celebrated at Easter.

Precatechumenate: A period of indeterminate length that precedes acceptance into the Order of Catechumens. In the *Rite of Christian Initiation of Adults*, this time is called the Period of Evangelization and Precate-chumenate; it is also referred to as inquiry.

Preparation Rites: Various rites that can be celebrated with the elect on Holy Saturday in proximate preparation for the celebration of the sacraments of initiation at the Easter Vigil that evening.

Presentations: Rites whereby the Church entrusts the Creed and the Lord's Prayer, the ancient texts that express the heart of the Church's faith, to the elect.

Proper: Those texts in the Mass and in the Liturgy of the Hours that are particular to a given day.

Purification and Enlightenment: The period of final preparation for unbaptized adults journeying toward for initiation in the Catholic Church. It is a time of intense spiritual preparation marked by the celebration of the Scrutinies and the Presentations. It usually coincides with Lent.

RCIA: *Rite of Christian Initiation of Adults,* the official rite of the Roman Catholic Church for initiation of adults and children of catechetical age and the reception of baptized candidates.

Reception of Baptized Christians into the Full Communion of the Catholic Church: The liturgical rite for receiving into the full communion of the Catholic Church an adult who was validly baptized in a non-Catholic Christian community.

Register of Catechumens: The book in which the names of those unbaptized adults who have been accepted as catechumens is recorded. The names of the sponsors and the minister and the date and place of the celebration of the *Rite of Acceptance into the Order of Catechumens* should also be recorded. Each parish should have a Register of Catechumens.

Renunciation of Sin: The ritual questioning that precedes the Profession of Faith made at Baptism or in the renewal of Baptism. There are two alternate forms of the formula for the renunciation of sin, each of which consists of three questions that center on the rejection of Satan and his works.

Rite of Baptism for Children: The ritual book that gives the rites for the Baptism of children who have not yet attained the age of discretion (the age of reason), presumed to be about age seven.

Rite of Christian Initiation of Adults (RCIA): The ritual book, part of the Roman Ritual, that gives the norms, directives, and ritual celebrations for initiating unbaptized adults and children who have reached catechetical age into Christ and incorporating them into the Church. The RCIA prescribes a sequence of periods and rites by which candidates transition from one stage to another, which culminate in the celebration of the sacraments of initiation, usually at the Easter Vigil.

Rite of Election: The second step for unbaptized adults preparing for the sacraments of initiation, also called the Enrollment of Names. The rite closes the period of the catechumenate and marks the beginning of the Period of Purification and Enlightenment, which usually corresponds to Lent. With this rite the Church makes its election, or choice, of the catechumens to receive the sacraments. The Rite of Election normally takes place on or near the First Sunday of Lent.

Sacraments of Christian Initiation: The Sacraments of Baptism, Confirmation, and Eucharist. All three sacraments are necessary to be fully initiated into the Church. Adults, including children of catechetical age, receive the three sacraments in one liturgy when being initiated into the Church.

Sacred Paschal Triduum: The three-day celebration of the Paschal Mystery of Christ that is the high point and center of the entire liturgical year. The Paschal Triduum begins with the Evening Mass of the Lord's Supper on Holy Thursday, solemnly remembers Christ's Death on Good Friday, reaches its zenith at the Easter Vigil with the Baptism of the elect into the mystery of Christ's Death and Resurrection, and concludes with Evening Prayer of Easter Sunday.

Scrutiny: A rite of self-searching and repentance intended to heal whatever is weak or sinful in the hearts of the elect, and to strengthen all that is good, in preparation for their reception of the Easter sacraments. The Scrutinies are exorcisms by which the elect are delivered from the power of Satan and protected against temptation. Usually three rites of Scrutiny are celebrated.

Sending of the Catechumens for Election: An optional rite that may be celebrated before the catechumens take part in the Rite of Election. The rite, which usually takes place at Mass, expresses the parish community's approval and support of the catechumens' election by the bishop.

Sponsor: In the Christian initiation of adults, one who accompanies a person seeking admission as a catechumen. The sponsor is someone who knows the candidate and is able to witness to the candidate's moral character, faith, and intention. He or she accompanies the candidate at the Rite of Acceptance into the Order of Catechumens and continues to accompany and support the person through the Period of the Catechumenate. In the celebration of the Sacrament of Confirmation with those who were baptized in infancy, the sponsor presents a person being confirmed to the minister of the sacrament. After the celebration of the sacrament, the sponsor helps the individual live in accord with their baptismal promises

White garment: The clothing, often similar to an alb, which is given to someone immediately after Baptism. This garment is a sign that the newly baptized person has put on new life in Christ. It is used in the Baptism of both adults and children.